Was Jesus a Capitalist?

Free Enterprise vs. Socialism

Jennifer B. Clark, Th.D.

Full Stature Ministries
Dennis and Dr. Jennifer Clark
Fort Mill, South Carolina
www.forgive123.com

www.xulonpress.com

*W*as *Jesus a Capitalist?* is a powerful, myth-busting book that confronts one of the central spiritual and political issues of our time. Dr. Jennifer Clark masterfully examines Biblical and historical evidence on the kind of economic system that fosters liberty and shatters bondage and dependence.

You need this book.

Your friends need this book.

Your country needs this book.

The time has come for a new birth of freedom! "

       – Jim Buchan, Crosslink Ministries

Jim Buchan has served a a pastor, an attorney, and the editor of MinistriesToday Magazine and The MorningStar Journal. His articles have appeared in more than 40 publications worldwide. Jim is the author of several books, including *Apostolic Evangelism* and *Walking the Leadership Highway—Without Becoming Road Kill!*

Dedication

*T*his book is dedicated to the children and youth of America. May you grasp the torch of liberty and guard it as though your life depends on it—for indeed it does.

A primary object. . . should be the education of our youth in the science of government. In a republic, what species of knowledge can be equally important? And what duty more pressing. . . than. . . communicating it to those who are to be the future guardians of the liberties of the country?
  –President George Washington, Eighth Annual Message to the Senate and House of Representatives, December 7, 1796

Contents

The moment the idea is admitted into society that property is not as sacred as the laws of God, and that there is not a force of law and public justice to protect it, anarchy and tyranny commence. If 'Thou shalt not covet' and 'Thou shalt not steal' were not commandments of Heaven, they must be made inviolable precepts in every society before it can be civilized or made free.

–John Adams, A Defense of the American Constitution, 1787

Chapter 1

GOOD NEWS OF FREEDOM

S ome ideas sound inspiring and look good on paper, but don't work well in real life. For example, suppose a man spent a lifetime studying birds in flight. He comes to believe that the key to flight lies in the motion of the wings. Other animals, he reasons, don't fly because they don't move their front legs or arms the right way.

After years of studying, drawing, and making calculations, he begins practicing. Day after day he spends hours flapping his arms like bird wings. Finally he is ready to climb up on the roof of a high building to test his theory. Would you advise him to jump? After all, he is very sincere. He believes that he has all the facts. However, he is *sincerely wrong*! In practice, his theory would fail miserably, perhaps with deadly consequences.

What about socialism, or even communism for that matter? Many people who have never experienced it in totality think that it sounds like a good idea. Ronald Reagan once said, "How can you tell a Communist? Well, it's someone who reads Marx and Lenin. How can you tell an anti-Communist? It's someone who understands Marx and Lenin."

Let's imagine how the concept of socialism might actually play out close to home to understand it better. Close to *your* home in fact. What would happen if *your* neighborhood formed a socialist government?

> ### *What would happen if your neighborhood formed a socialist government?*

A socialist/communist neighborhood

Let's suppose that your neighborhood HOA (Home Owners Association) says it is not fair for some neighbors to have more than others. They tell you that you have been unfairly treated and deserve more. They point out that some neighbors live in mansions, but most live in much smaller houses.

You begin to be envious of your richer neighbors and want what they have. The HOA promises you that if they were in charge, they would take from the rich to give you everything you need. They promise to right the economic wrongs. "It's all about equality," the HOA exclaims.

Wait! What vital point are you missing here? Aren't you even slightly skeptical about the claims made by television commercials or car salesmen? You know that they are not looking out for *your* best interests, they just want to sell you something.

When individuals are promised better housing, great retirement benefits, never-ending unemployment insurance, and all the various entitlements provided by the government, it is truly astounding that people actually *believe* the politicians are really looking out for them. Consider the riots in Greece and England in 2011. The governments were going broke, they couldn't keep their promises, and the people rioted to demand entitlements to which they had grown accustomed.

As Margaret Thatcher once declared, "Socialist governments. . . always run out of other people's money."[1]

Socialist governments always run out of other people's money!

Question! Question their motives. Question their honesty. Remember that the words "crooked" and "politician" are paired together for a reason. Start asking, "Why?" Why are they promising you this? Are they *really* concerned about you? Are they truly so altruistic, so compassionate, so generous that they are only thinking about your welfare? Or do they have a *hidden agenda* you are overlooking? Is there a possibility that you are being. . .conned? Now, back to the neighborhood:

- *You give up your rights and freedoms and grant the HOA power to control the neighborhood economy. You vote them into POWER to "right the wrongs!"*

- *"From each according to ability, to each according to need," the HOA says. Everyone thinks, "I'll get all I need!" and imagines living in a wonderful utopia.*

- *Everyone gives their property to the HOA so they can redistribute the wealth of the neighborhood in a more equitable way.*

- *The HOA, however, takes most of it to run the government, pay their employees, and make sure they get big paychecks and really nice vacations. And they themselves move into the nicest houses after evicting the original owners. After all, "Everyone is equal but some are more equal than others!"* (**Animal Farm** *by George Orwell.*)

- *The HOA decides your house is too big for your family, so they move in four other families.*

- *You still get the same as your neighbors, even if you work harder; so everyone cuts back and less is produced. Rationing begins.*

- *The HOA decides you are using too much electricity, so they only allow you to turn on the lights for two hours a day.*

- *The HOA decides that individuals older than sixty-five are too old to do enough work, and are using up resources that could benefit more productive neighbors in the collective. So, for the good of the neighborhood, the HOA comes to the conclusion that the elderly must be euthanized. Does that seem shocking? Read this quote by a famous socialist.*

George Bernard Shaw (1856-1950), Irish playwright, co-founder of the London School of Economics and Fabian Socialist, stated:

The moment we face it frankly, we are driven to the conclusion that the community has a right to put a price on the right to live in it. . .If people are fit to live, let them live under decent human conditions. If they are not fit to live, kill them in a decent human way. Is it any wonder that some of us are driven to prescribe the lethal chamber as the solution for the hard cases which are at present made the excuse for dragging all the other cases down to their level, and the only solution that will create a sense of full social responsibility in modern populations?[2]

The Big Lie: "You can get something for nothing."

Too many people believe the Big Lie without questioning it for three main reasons:

The Big Lie: "You can get something for nothing."

First, people get hooked by their own greed. Greed is a selfish and excessive desire for more of something than is needed (such as money or possessions). If two small children are asked to choose between two pieces of unevenly sliced cake, each will invariably want the larger slice. It is just human nature to be greedy.

Advertising campaigns use greed and lust to sell cars. A commercial shows a person pulling up with a nice new Brand X car, with all the neighbors looking at it enviously. This is manipulation. The marketers are appealing to your baser appetites, not your higher nature. Politicians use the tool of *class envy*. They deliberately stir up greed by pointing out certain groups of people who have more than others. The politicians then promise to "take from the rich to give to the poor." This manipulative strategy was used by President Franklin D. Roosevelt to get Americans to agree to the income tax.

The 1935 Act was popularly known at the time as the "Soak the Rich" tax. Did the income tax really soak just the rich, or did it soak everyone, including you? That's how they trick the people. Who gets to spend the money? The politicians! Ironically, charities have to work much harder than politicians because moving people to feel *compassion* is much more difficult than causing them to *sin*.

Second, some people are lazy and like the idea of living off others so they don't have to work. Would you voluntarily cut your own grass if you thought someone else would do it *for* you? Would a child voluntarily clean his own room if mom always did it for him? It is just human nature to be irresponsible.

Parents have to *teach* a child to have a good work ethic. It doesn't come naturally. Do children become more grateful, or more demanding when they become dependent? Would they treat their mother with respect if she became a slave to their every whim, or would they become domineering despots?

Benjamin Franklin had observed firsthand the destructive effects of socialism and welfare dependency in England. He said it created people who are "idle, dissolute, drunken, and insolent," and took from them "all inducements to industry, frugality, and sobriety."

I am for doing good to the poor, but I differ in opinion of the means. I think the best way of doing good to the poor, is not making them easy in poverty, but leading or driving them out of it. In my youth I travelled much, and I observed in different countries, that the more public provisions were made for the poor, the less they provided for themselves, and of course became poorer. And, on the contrary, the less was done for them, the more they did for themselves, and became richer.

–Benjamin Franklin, On The London Chronicle,
November 29, 1766

Finally, some really believe the ideology of socialism/communism is fair and noble. These idealists, however, seldom study the historical evidence to see if it has ever worked. Failing to truly understand human nature, they envision only the beauty of the ideal.

They fantasize, "Wouldn't it be just wonderful if people would just get along, share everything with everyone else, be compliant workers for the collective, and do everything their leaders tell them to do?"

> ### *If men were angels, no government would be necessary.*

Wow! That sounds a lot like how parents dream about home life and their children. "Wouldn't it be lovely if everyone would just stop fighting, stop wanting their own way, and our teenagers would do what they are told?" Yes, it certainly would be wonderful. What a lovely fantasy! Then everyone would be just like Mother Theresa! However, it is just human nature to be selfish and rebellious. Nice dream, but not very likely. People are *not* angels. James Madison, the Father of the Constitution, said:

If men were angels, no government would be necessary. If angels were to govern men, neither external nor internal controls on government would be necessary.

–The Federalist 51, Independent Journal, February 6, 1778

The socialists/communists believe several things that are fundamentally contrary to scripture. They actually believe that man is good and civilization makes man bad. Therefore, if they can restructure society, man's goodness can emerge. However, our Founding Fathers had no delusions about the sinful bent of the human heart.

They understood that men are *not* angels. Those in the general population must be governed by law, and those in power must be restrained or they will become tyrants. The Founders knew that men are sinners, and they become greedy for wealth and power.

The socialists and communists are also convinced they alone are the enlightened ones who must construct the ideal society through social engineering, because the ordinary people are too stupid to construct this utopia by themselves. They divide mankind into two classes: the ruling elite and the stupid herd. They view themselves as the wise ranchers and the ignorant people as a herd of cattle that they must control. [3,4]

The Founding Fathers respected men as those who were created in the image of God, even though they were flawed by sin. The Founders believed that God gave men rights and civil government should protect those rights. America's Founders believed that a people who lived in humility under the rule of God and His precepts could govern their own lives and then govern the government. This was the great American experiment. "Can man govern himself?"

> **The great American experiment:**
> **"Can man govern himself?"**

The Terrible Truth: You trade your freedom for *slavery!*

What would a ruling elite possibly get out of having power to control the wealth?

Power and wealth for *themselves*, of course! Even if they sincerely believe in the ideology, do you honestly think they *really* care about individuals? The truth is that they want to make you so afraid to lose your entitlements that you would keep voting them into office! They promise you things, and you become part of their voting base. If you don't vote for them, you lose your benefits. Even if they supply less and less, they still rule you through fear. It is a trap. You become their. . .slave!

> *Fear is the foundation of most governments.*
>
>   –John Adams, Thoughts on Government, 1776

Good news of freedom

Jesus came to set the captives free. He proclaimed the good news of freedom to all mankind. Why should we allow ourselves to become enslaved to any man or government when Jesus came to set us free from slavery? However, it is important to realize that Jesus came not to set us free *from* civil government, but to reveal His freedom formula *for* godly civil government.

When Jesus stood in the synagogue at the beginning of His ministry, He read from Isaiah 61:1-2, proclaiming the heart of who Jesus is, and His mission for mankind as the anointed One, the Christ.

The Spirit of the Lord is upon Me,

Because He has anointed Me

To preach the gospel to the poor;

He has sent Me to heal the brokenhearted,

To proclaim liberty to the captives

And recovery of sight to the blind,

To set at liberty those who are oppressed;

To proclaim the acceptable year of the Lord [emphasis mine]

(Luke 4:18).

How many people think of "liberty to the captives" and "liberty for the oppressed" as individual salvation? Is there a "collective salvation"? Not in the same way taught by liberation theology, which is just another flavor of Marxism. Collective salvation has nothing to do with faith, or Christ, or spiritual salvation. It just means forming a socialist or communist "collective" community or nation for forced income equality. God is indeed concerned about nations as well as individual salvation, but His ideas are vastly different. Father God promised His Son the nations of the earth. The day will come when entire nations will be judged by God as goat or sheep nations.

I will declare the decree:

The Lord has said to Me,

'You are My Son,

Today I have begotten You.

Ask of Me, and I will give You

The nations for Your inheritance,

And the ends of the earth for Your possession (Psalm 2:7-9).

When the Son of Man comes in His glory, and all the holy angels with Him, then He will sit on the throne of His glory. All the nations will be gathered before Him, and He will separate them one from another, as a shepherd divides his sheep from the goats (Matthew 25:31-32).

In Isaiah 9:6-8, we are told the Lord Jesus Christ will bring His government and peace to the earth and He will order and establish His kingdom with judgment and justice:

For unto us a Child is born,

Unto us a Son is given;

And the government will be upon His shoulder.

And His name will be called

Wonderful, Counselor, Mighty God,

Everlasting Father, Prince of Peace.

Of the increase of His government and peace

There will be no end,

Upon the throne of David and over His kingdom,

To order it and establish it with judgment and justice

From that time forward, even forever.

The zeal of the Lord of hosts will perform this.

These verses are not talking about someday in heaven or during the 1,000-year Millennial Reign of Christ, but the Lord actually governing on earth in the nations. Has this ever happened in a whole nation before? Yes, twice. God ruled in the nation of Israel and God established civil government in America. America was dedicated to God by the French Huguenots (1565 at Fort Caroline, Florida) to become a dwelling place for God (Psalm 132:1-5).

In 1620, the Pilgrims at Plymouth, Massachusetts, made a covenant and established civil government under God through the Mayflower Compact. The Founding Fathers of America acknowledged this holy calling.

The general principles on which the fathers achieved independence were the general principles of Christianity. I will avow that I then believed, and now believe, that those general principles of Christianity are as eternal and immutable as the existence and attributes of God.

–John Adams, letter to Thomas Jefferson,

June 28, 1813

It cannot be emphasized too strongly or too often that this great nation was founded, not by religionists, but by Christians; not on religion, but on the gospel of Jesus Christ. For this very reason peoples of other faiths have been afforded asylum, prosperity, and freedom of worship here.

–Patrick Henry, The Trumpet Voice of Freedom, p. iii.

Jesus concluded His mission statement by announcing that He was ushering in the age of Jubilee for all men, "the acceptable year of the Lord." During the Year of Jubilee, once every fifty years, all Israelites who had sold themselves into slavery were set free, and all land that had been sold reverted to its original owner. However, Jesus came to bring Jubilee, freedom, to all mankind. God is the author of freedom. He proclaimed liberty through His Son and breathed the desire for freedom into the hearts of men everywhere — a God-initiated "yearning to be free."

America's Founding Fathers were architects of a brand new form of government.

Our Founding Fathers were architects of a brand new form of government: A nation of FREEMEN where the people would not be owned by the government, but would "govern" the government.

The political spectrum

In America, we often talk about the left and right sides of a political spectrum. The left ranges from liberals to socialists to communists at the farthest left. Conservatives are placed on the right side of the scale, with Nazis at the farthest right of the right wing. However, this doesn't make any sense, because Nazis (National *Socialists*) were actually just a slightly different flavor of the far left. What, then, is in the center? Halfway between two forms of totalitarianism? And how can those who love freedom be on the same side of the scale as a dictatorship?

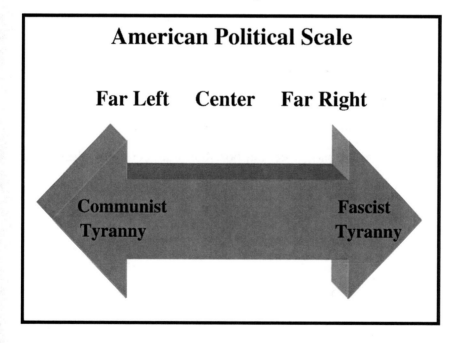

American Political Scale

Far Left   **Center**   **Far Right**

Communist
Tyranny

Fascist
Tyranny

"People's Law"

Excessive government is tyranny. Too little government results in anarchy. Tyranny and anarchy are true opposites. Anarchy never lasts long, because the people begin crying out for protection and stability. And a tyrant inevitably arises to take control. Following the French Revolution, the nation devolved into chaos. Within ten years, Napoleon became emperor. France swung from anarchy to tyranny again in a very short period of time.

Our Founding Fathers used a different, more accurate, scale. They judged politics and governments according to *freedom*. Tyranny was cruel and oppressive while anarchy was violent and unstable. One was *total* law, the other was *no* law. 100 percent law on one side and 0 percent law on the other. So true freedom would be somewhere between total law and no law.

The Founders were looking for the **balanced center,** where men could live in the most freedom possible, but society would still be ordered and stable without sliding into either tyranny or anarchy. Thomas Jefferson called this balanced center **People's Law**.

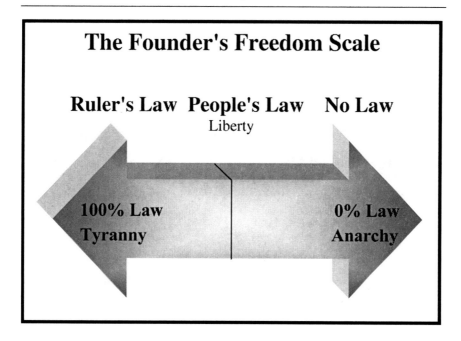

Governing the government

How could the governed actually *govern the government?* Was there a way for the people to elect representatives, live under the rule of law, preserve their rights and freedom, and prevent the government from seizing excessive power?

The essence of Government is power; and power, lodged as it must be in human hands, will ever be liable to abuse. –James Madison, speech in the Virginia constitutional convention, December 2, 1829

29

The Declaration of Independence states that government must exercise power by the consent of the people. Government should not exercise power over the people. The U.S. Constitution, the Supreme Law of the Land in the United States of America, begins with these words: **WE THE PEOPLE**. What an amazing concept! Government works for us, we don't work for it. The government is *our* servant, and we are not its slaves. People's Law!

Governments are instituted among men, deriving their just powers from the consent of the governed.

–Declaration of Independence, July 4, 1776

Here sir, the people govern.

–Alexander Hamilton, speech, New York Ratifying Convention, June 17, 1788

Chapter One

Discussion Questions

1. What is the "Big Lie" and why do people believe it?
2. What did James Madison mean by the statement: "If men were angels, no government would be necessary"?

3. The socialists and communists believe they can construct an ideal society. How do they view their role and what is their view of the common man?

4. Describe the Founding Fathers' beliefs about mankind.

5. Define "individual salvation" and "collective salvation." What is the difference between the two?

6. Is God concerned about nations?

7. What are the differences between the current American political spectrum and the Founders' Freedom Scale?

8. What is "Peoples' Law"? What is "the balanced center"?

9. What are the two extremes of law?

10. According to the Founder's, what is the purpose of government?

Chapter 2

THE BIG PICTURE

*H*ave you ever heard the saying "they can't see the forest for the trees"? It is a reference to individuals who are so focused on details that they can't see the big picture. Most people see only what is happening in life around them, the current issues of the day.

Many students dislike history because it is presented as facts and dates to memorize and they don't understand its relevance for current events. Without a frame of reference, there seems to be no continuity or purpose in the details. The purpose of this chapter is to give you the big picture — total concept. If you learn history this way, you will be able to understand the past and current events with much greater clarity.

Advancing freedom

In the past 2,000 years, since the birth of the Church on the day of Pentecost, God has not stopped working. His kingdom has continued to expand on earth, but not without great opposition. It is far too much to cover in depth in this book, but studying the details of history within the context of God's plan for restoration greatly increases overall comprehension of civil and religious history. Consider the big picture from the context of scripture:

*Repent therefore and be converted, that our sins may be blotted out, so that times of refreshing may come from the presence of the Lord, and that He may send Jesus Christ, who was preached to you before, whom heaven must receive until **the times of RESTORATION of all things, which God has spoken by the mouth of all His holy prophets since the world began** [emphasis mine] (Acts 3:19-21).*

Acts 3:19-21 tells us a couple of very significant truths. First, we can expect God to send times of refreshing, or revival. The history of America can be set within the context of continuous cycles of repentance and revival. God not only birthed America in covenant, but continually turned the heart of America back to Himself through times of awakening.

Not just in America, but throughout all history, God has expanded His kingdom in orchestrated movements of His Spirit. At an appointed time, God sets the stage, chooses a man or a people, and moves in the nations. Some examples include the Protestant Reformation, the Pietist Movement, the Holiness Movement with John and Charles Wesley, and the First and Second Great Awakenings in America. Second, these verses state that Jesus will return only after the "times of the restoration of all things spoken by the mouth of all His holy prophets since the world began."

> *God sets the stage, chooses a man or a people, and moves in the nations.*

The **Advancing Freedom** diagram spans 2,000 years, from the birth of the Church on Pentecost, around 30 AD, to the present. The timeline at the top of the diagram is a linear timeline of 2,000 years. In accordance with God's plan of restoration, the Advancing Freedom timeline (pages 35-36) represents the downward deterioration of the Church and civilization for a thousand years, until 1,000 AD, the Midnight of the Dark Ages. There was a period of deterioration, but we are now in a time of restoration of what was lost.

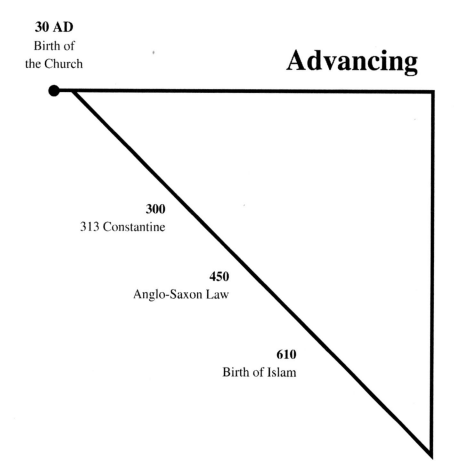

30 AD
Birth of
the Church

Advancing

300
313 Constantine

450
Anglo-Saxon Law

610
Birth of Islam

1000
Midnight of
Dark Ages

Freedom

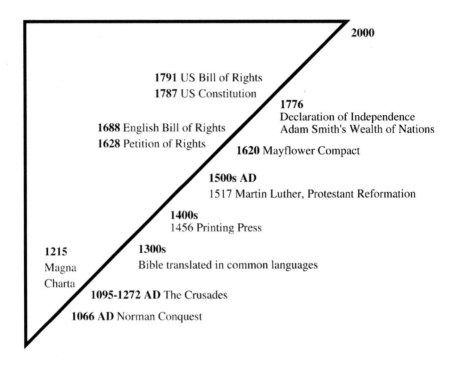

However, even during the deterioration in the Dark Ages, God had lights in the monasteries, and lights such as the Desert Fathers, St. Polycarp, Cyprian of Carthage, St. Denis, and evangelists such as St. Patrick, St. Augustine, and many others. Every generation had its remnant who experienced the deep things of God, although truth was hidden from the majority.

God will complete what He has planned to accomplish. All His intentions, everything God's prophets have prophesied, will be expressed in perfect fullness. Anything the enemy has ever thwarted or the hand of man has corrupted will come to a final and glorious culmination. All things will be restored. It may seem like God is taking a long time, but it is brief in the context of eternity. From 1000 AD to the present day, restoration has been occurring at a more and more rapid pace.

> *You must not forget this one thing, dear friends: A day is like a thousand years to the Lord, and a thousand years is like a day. The Lord isn't really being slow about his promise, as some people think. No, he is being patient for your sake (2 Peter 3:8-9 NLT).*

The Bible, which was formerly reserved almost exclusively for monks and priests of the Catholic Church, was translated into the common languages of the people by men such as John Wycliffe (1320-1384) and John Hus (1369-1415) in the 14th century. In 1456, Johannes Gutenberg invented the printing press and the very first book printed was the Bible. Suddenly, ordinary believers had access to a Bible they could read in their own languages.

Martin Luther (1483-1546), a German priest and professor of theology who disagreed with the practice of indulgences, ushered in the Protestant Reformation when he nailed his 95 Theses to the Wittenburg church door in 1517. The truth that "the just are saved by faith" was restored to the Church. People didn't have to work for salvation, or earn salvation, but must simply believe and receive by faith. Many other movements have since brought further restoration of lost truths to the Church.

How could men be free?

The second book of the Bible, Exodus, tells the story of the enslavement of the children of Israel by the Pharaoh of Egypt, and their release from bondage after 400 years. The Israelites cried out for deliverance and God sent a deliverer, Moses, to lead them out. However, the author of liberty, Jesus Christ, has *continued* His freedom mission by inaugurating civil freedom in government.

> *Jesus has continued His freedom mission by inaugurating civil freedom in government.*

When Thomas Jefferson studied history searching for examples of freedom in civil government, he found a type in ancient Israel. He studied the biblical account in Exodus in which Moses' father-in-law, Jethro, suggested a plan of government which Jefferson considered to be a form of People's Law (Exodus 18:20-26).

Jefferson was searching for an ideal balance of civil government so men could be free, yet not slide into tyranny or anarchy. No such government had ever been planned out before. There was no blueprint to follow. It could not be copied, it could only be invented.

How *could* men be free? There were almost no examples of freemen. But far across the Atlantic Ocean, explorers had discovered a land of refuge. During the turbulent religious wars between the 12th to 18th centuries, multitudes fled from persecution. Many came to the safe haven of colonial America to find freedom of religion.

Since the 1600s, the clergy preached about liberty from the pulpits of America. Civil leaders such as Thomas Hooker of Hartford, Connecticut, experimented at town and state level with forms of free government. The colonists had spoken and written of liberty, the God-given rights of man, and the duties and purposes of government. Long before the Revolutionary War, the flame of independence was already burning in the hearts of the American colonists.

Historical examples

When Thomas Jefferson pored over historical accounts, he found only one other clear example of *People's Law* in history, besides that of Moses in the book of Exodus. In the unlikely location of the British Isles, a small group of Anglo-Saxons devised a system of civil government very similar to the system that Jethro suggested to Moses. They even called the leader of a group of ten, who exercised certain legal responsibilities and authority, a "tythingman."

How could principles from scripture have been discovered by these tribes? Some have hypothesized that they were descendants of the Lost Tribes of Israel, who migrated north to Assyria and eventually reached the British Isles, where they founded a society based on the precepts of the Word of God.

> ***Thomas Jefferson discover two examples of People's Law in history: ancient Israel under Moses and the Anglo-Saxons.***

Advancing freedom in civil government

A progressive restoration of freedom can be observed from 1000 AD onward. Following the Norman Conquest in Great Britain in 1066 AD, Englishmen struggled to regain freedom. Those who fled to America had the same fire.

Thomas Jefferson saw that the basis of English common law was established with the arrival of Anglo-Saxon tribes under the leadership of the tribal chiefs Hengist and Horsa in 450 AD. Common law is the ancient law of England based on the customs of society according to the negative golden rule—don't do unto others what you would not have them do unto you. Common law was recognized and enforced by the judgments and decrees of the courts.

An innate sense of liberty was planted in the hearts of Englishmen from the outset. The Norman Conquest had suppressed liberty, but failed to suspend the impetus for freedom.

The cause of liberty and the "natural rights of Englishmen" once again progressed with the granting of Magna Charta in 1215, a rudimentary Parliament in 1264, Petition of Rights in 1628, and English Bill of Rights in 1688. The struggle for freedom was long and often violent. Many of the oppressed fled to the American colonies for asylum, and the refugees cherished within their hearts the yearning for liberty.

Jefferson was convinced that the form of government being formed in the emerging United States was a restoration of the sublime Anglo-Saxon principles. It was now North America at the forefront of liberty.

Freedom burst into full bloom in the American colonies with the signing of the Declaration of Independence in 1776, and later in the U.S. Constitution, which was ratified in 1789, replacing the Articles of Confederation. A new form of government was born, a true example of liberty for all the world to see.

The Wealth of Nations

Another significant event occurred in 1776. *The Wealth of Nations,* by Adam Smith, was published. Freedom was paired with the blueprint for a prosperous national economy based on free enterprise. Smith wrote that prosperity requires only peace, low taxes, and a good system of justice—the rule of law. The principal theme of *The Wealth of Nations* is that a nation promotes its own wealth most advantageously through having a framework of laws leaving individuals free to pursue the healthy self-interest they have in their own economic success.

> ***Two key events for America occurred in 1776: The Declaration of Independence was signed and The Wealth of Nations was published.***

Four Key Epochs of History

Military Might: pre-history-300 AD

During the first epoch of history, military might was the predominant force vying for control in the earth. This was the time of military leaders such as Alexander the Great, Genghis Khan, Cyrus the Great of Persia, and the Caesars of Rome. In the 2nd century AD, four world empires formed and dominated the known world: the Roman, Parthian, Kushan, and Han Chinese. Barbarians then overran the civilized empires, bringing this epoch to an end.

Religion: 300 -1715

Religion shaped the known world during this time, spreading influence through evangelism (Christianity), exploration, and religious wars. Catholicism, Protestantism, and Islam struggled for control. Islam and Christianity warred over the control of the Holy Land and Europe. Constantine (227 AD - 337 AD), who was Roman emperor from 306 AD - 337 AD, became the first Christian emperor. He had a vision of the Cross of Christ on the battlefield, and subsequently helped develop the Edict of Milan, which protected Christians from persecution.

The Crusades (1095 AD -1291 AD) were military expeditions undertaken to deliver the Holy Land from Muslim tyranny and occupation. Later, a remnant of knights successfully repelled the Muslim armies who sought to invade and conquer Europe itself. During this time, Catholicism also warred against Protestantism.

Religious wars included the French Wars of Religion in the 16th century and the Thirty Years War in the early 17th century (German states, Scandinavia, Poland).

Politics: 1215 - 1900

From the time of the Magna Charta in 1215 through 1900, governments warred against one another. The great struggle within the British Isles was for the rights and freedom of individuals. The American colonies fought for and gained independence in the American Revolution, establishing a new form of government that became a freedom model for the world.

The French rebelled against the ruling aristocracy in the French Revolution (1789), but after slaughtering 16,000-40,000 of their own citizens in the Reign of Terror (1793-1794) and ten years of chaos, they reverted to tyranny under the rule of Napoleon.

Economics: Present Day

The war being waged in the present is a war for economic control. The three economic forces vying for domination are free enterprise, socialism/communism, and Sharia law. Free enterprise, or capitalism, requires peace, rule of law, and a low level of government regulation. It is a system of minimal control and maximum opportunity to succeed.

- Free Enterprise
- Socialism/Communism
- Islamic Sharia Law (government and economic system). The goal is economic jihad to bring the world under Sharia for global dominance.

Capitalism: Teach a man to fish

- The poor get an education and work hard.
- Many of the poor become part of the middle class.
- The middle class becomes larger and everyone benefits.
- The middle class gets more education and works hard.
- The middle class becomes richer.
- Some from the middle class become rich.

> ***Any government that uses coercion to confiscate the property of its citizens is greedy and selfish.***

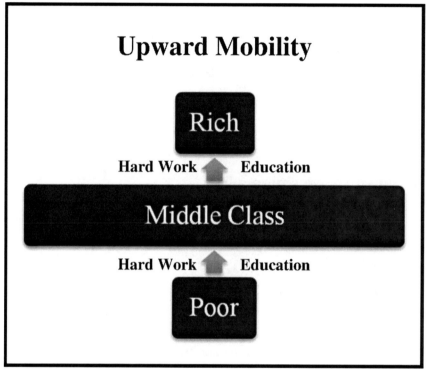

A free economy makes it possible for individuals to move up to a higher social and economic position.

Socialism is a system in which ownership of industry and distribution of wealth are determined by the government. Socialism/communism requires manipulation, coercion, or deadly force to seize and keep power. Although the concept of socialism/communism can be traced back to ancient philosophers, Karl Marx (1818-1883) and Friedrich Engels (1820-1895) believed in the necessity of violent revolution to bring true governmental change.

In the present day, progressives, socialists, communists, Marxists, liberals, and populists all want the same thing—socialism/communism. They call themselves different names, but the goal is still the same. Most want to bring change slowly by small incremental steps through legislation and regulation. The more radical members of the movement are committed to the use of violence to gain power, seize property, and force collectivization.

Socialism: Give a man a fish

- Tax the rich and middle class to give to the government.
- The government is greedy.
- The government keeps most of the money for itself.
- The government gives some money for handouts.
- The poor use the handouts and then need more handouts.
- The economy gets worse.
- The middle class shrinks and the poor get poorer.

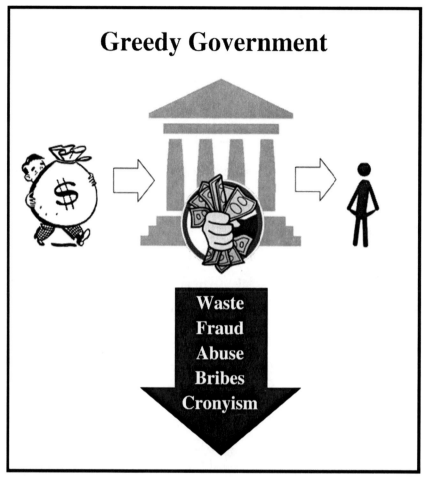

Government cannot create wealth. All it can do is consume wealth. Ronald Reagan once said, "Government is not a solution to our problem, government is the problem."

Businessmen who want to make a profit aren't greedy. Individuals who believe they have a right to keep their own property aren't greedy. So, who *is* greedy and selfish? Anyone who wants to take possessions belonging to another person is greedy and selfish. Any government that uses coercion to confiscate the property of its citizens is greedy and selfish.

> ## *Capitalism: Teach a man to fish. Socialism: Give a man a fish.*

Crony capitalism

Unfortunately, when *enterprise* is no longer *free*, and business gets in cahoots with the government, a toxic brew of *crony capitalism* results. Crony capitalism is not capitalism at all. Favor is earned and manipulated by political posturing based on mutual advantage. A shared monopoly develops which grants unfair advantage to the favored few, bestows special privileges and tax concessions, and runs competitors out of business. Government collects taxes from *citizens* to give subsidies and make favorable loans to pet companies (such as Solyndra, the now defunct solar panel company).

Crony capitalism harms both consumers and the general economy. It benefits *only* government and cronies. Any government that manipulates business for its own benefit is greedy and selfish.

It was not bad theory alone that caused the [financial crisis of 2008]. A clutch of the top executives of our greatest banks joined with fly-by-night mortgage brokers and august agencies of the government in an unspoken conspiracy of fraud, with their own institutions among the ultimate victims. While the fraud was happening it was winked at and even encouraged by nearly every relevant regulatory and political authority, with a few ineffectual exceptions. The ideology was essential to the deceptions that, had they appeared in their raw and rabid form, might have been resisted.[1]

If, from the more wretched parts of the old world, we look at those which are in an advanced stage of improvement, we still find the greedy hand of government thrusting itself into every corner and crevice of industry, and grasping the spoil of the multitude. Invention is continually exercised, to furnish new pretenses for revenues and taxation. It watches prosperity as its prey and permits none to escape without tribute.

–Thomas Paine, Rights of Man, 1791

Chapter Two

Discussion Questions

1. What does the "restoration of all things" mean in the context of freedom and civil government?

2. Thomas Jefferson searched history for examples of People's Law. What two examples did he find?

3. What role might the Lost Tribes of Israel have played as far as civil government in the British Isles?

4. How could a history of freedom have impacted the struggle to regain freedom following the Norman Conquest?

5. How significant was the signing of The Declaration of Independence and publishing *The Wealth of Nations* occurred simultaneously?

6. Describe the four key epochs of history. What is the present day battle?

7. What would be the benefit of teaching a man to fish rather than just giving a man a fish?

8. What does "upward mobility" mean in terms of economics and social class?

9. Why is "crony capitalism" damaging to free enterprise?

Chapter 3

TEST BY THE SOURCE

*T*he source of life determines what will grow. Orange trees grow oranges, grape vines grow grapes. A *source* is the start, beginning, root, or origin of something. Every concept, philosophy, point of view, religion, and belief has a source.

Two kingdoms, two sources

The physical world was created from the *spiritual* realm. God spoke and the sun, moon, earth, stars, solar systems, and galaxies were created out of tiny particles of energy held together by the power of God, with the spiritual having dominion over the natural.

In many separate revelations [each of which set forth a portion of the Truth] and in different ways God spoke of old to [our] fore-fathers in and by the prophets, [But] in the last of these days He has spoken to us in [the person of a] Son, Whom He appointed Heir and lawful Owner of all things, also by and through Whom He created the worlds and the reaches of space and the ages of time [He made, produced, built, operated, and arranged them in order]. He is the sole expression of the glory of God [the Light-being, the out-raying or radiance of the divine], and He is the perfect imprint and very image of [God's]nature, upholding and maintaining and guiding and propelling the universe by His mighty word of power. . . (Hebrews 1:3 AMP).

In Genesis, the book of beginnings, we are told God created the physical universe. With the fall of man, another spiritual kingdom, the kingdom of the devil, began to influence what God created, and the epic battle of the two kingdoms began. The source of everything in the spiritual realm is one of two kingdoms. In the Garden of Eden, God said that everything He had created was good. Why? Because God is good so only good comes from Him. The source determines the outcome.

Then God saw everything that He had made, and indeed it was very good (Genesis 1:31).

God gave Adam and Eve the title deed and dominion on the earth He had created.

Then God blessed them, and God said to them, "Be fruitful and multiply; fill the earth and subdue it; have dominion over the fish of the sea, over the birds of the air, and over every living thing that moves on the earth" (Genesis 1:28).

However, at the fall of man when sin entered, the created world came under the control of the enemy. Matter itself is not evil, but the wind behind it is either good or evil, either God or the devil, depending on how it is used.

We know that we are of God, and the whole world lies under the sway of the wicked one (1 John 5:19).

When the kingdom of God is the source, the end result will be the fruit of love, life, prosperity, and freedom. If the kingdom of the devil is the source, fear, death, poverty, and captivity will ultimately be expressed. Philosophy, art, music, literature, economics, and all other reflections of society have a spiritual force behind them for either good or evil. Nothing originates from a vacuum. Each economic theory comes from one of these two kingdoms. The source is either the kingdom of God or the kingdom of the devil.

Kingdom of God	Kingdom of the Devil
Love	Fear
Life (Zoë)	Death
Prosperity	Poverty
Freedom	Captivity

Wealth

God created an earth with plentiful and amazing wealth. The Bible says that wealth belongs to God, but man is steward of it.

The earth is the LORD's, and the fullness thereof; the world, and they that dwell therein (Psalm 24:1 KJV).

'The silver is Mine, and the gold is Mine,' says the LORD of hosts (Haggai 2:8).

Under the surface of the earth there are tremendous amounts of resources like minerals, coal, oil, and natural gas. There are animals on the ground, in the air, and in the seas. God blessed us with a multitude of trees and plants with seeds to continually supply us with cycles of natural renewal. The Bible tells us that God also has given man the ability to create wealth with these resources.

Remember the LORD your God, for it is He who gives you power [ability] to get wealth (Deuteronomy 8:18).

Wealth consists of many things, including natural resources. God also created precious metals and gemstones. Wealth was God's idea, and it is so important to Him that He gives ample instruction about the right way and wrong way to use finances.

Economics is the study of how people choose to use resources.

From Genesis to Revelation, depending on the translation, the Bible refers to gold and silver more than 700 times. Gold is mentioned in the scriptures more often than any other metal. The word *money* refers to gold and silver, which were used for currency in biblical times. In the King James Version of the Bible, gold is mentioned 417 times and silver 320 times.

Wealth includes:

- Land
- Gold, silver, precious stones
- Material goods and natural resources
- Creativity (Creator God, Spirit of the Creator)

Creativity is included as wealth because it is the source of literature, music, art, scientific advances, witty inventions, technology, and so forth, which benefit mankind.

Economics

Economics is the study of how people choose to use resources. It explains the production and consumption of goods, and the exchange and transfer of wealth for producing and obtaining goods. Economics describes the interaction of people within markets to get products or services they need or to accomplish particular goals. Since economics is a driving force of human interaction, studying it can reveal why people and governments behave in certain ways.

> *Wealth was God's idea.*

The two main types of economics are microeconomics and macroeconomics. Microeconomics considers the actions of individuals and industries, such as the dynamics between buyers and sellers, borrowers and lenders. Macroeconomics analyzes the economic activity of a whole nation or the international marketplace. The history of macroeconomics reveals how economic theory and practice has changed from the ancient times to present day.

- **Barter**

Bartering is the exchange of goods and services without the use of currency. Popularly used in ancient times, it has been a common method of exchange in societies or social situations marked by a low or non-existent money supply.

- **Currency, coins and paper money**

Around 1200 BC, cowrie shells began to be used as a medium of exchange. Cowries are the most widely and longest used currency in history. From around 1000 BC, primitive coins were manufactured from base metals, and around 500 BC, coins were made from silver, bronze, and gold. In 806-1455 AD, paper currency began to be used in China, and was used in Europe after 1151 AD.

- **Manorialism** (400 AD-1400 AD)

Manorialism was a political, economic, and social system in medieval Europe. A manor consisted of a large main house for the lord of the manor, one or more villages, and up to several thousand surrounding acres. Manors, not villages, were the economic and social units of life in the early Middle Ages. Peasants were tied to the land under control of a lord. By 1000 AD, most peasants had become serfs, or semi-slaves, because of debt.

Feudalism (800 AD –1400 AD)

Feudalism was a hierarchical system in which a lord or king gave a gift or land (known in Latin as a *feudum*) to a vassal, or knight, in exchange for protection.

Since feudal Europe depended heavily on agriculture, wealth came from land. Land ownership became a way to improve social status and become a member of the upper class.

Fiefs were granted to a vassal only for the lifetime of that vassal, but it was common for a son to inherit a father's title. This practice was called primogeniture. The decline of feudalism began during the time of the Crusades, when a demand was put on the production of goods and a money system was developed.

• **Mercantilism** (1600 AD–1800 AD)

Mercantilism is an economic system in which government control of foreign trade was considered of utmost importance to ensure the prosperity and security of a state.

It was based on the accumulation of gold, gaining colonies, maintaining a merchant marine, as well as developing industry and mining for a favorable balance of trade. Wealth could only be accumulated, not created. Mercantilism dominated Western Europe from the 17th to the late 18th century. Mercantilism was a cause of frequent European wars in that time. It was also a motive for colonial expansion.

• **Free Enterprise**

Free enterprise is an economic system in which private businesses are free to operate competitively for profit with minimal government regulation, interference, or subsidy. It is governed by the law of supply and demand and regulated by competition. The word *capitalism* was coined by Karl Marx as a derogatory term for free enterprise.

> *Karl Marx: Socialism is merely a step on the way to communism.*

• **Socialism/communism**

Socialism is an economic and political system where money and goods are shared collectively, supposedly for the common good. According to socialists/communists, the wealth of a society must be shared, and everyone in it will have all they need. Individual rights, property, and needs cannot be more important than the needs of everyone else.

Karl Marx said socialism is merely a *step* on the way to communism.

False premise of socialism

Socialism is based on a *false premise* that there is a certain fixed amount of wealth that must be redistributed for everyone to get an equitable share. Redistribution of wealth requires coerced taking from some to give to others. This is theft. Free enterprise is the only economic system that allows more wealth to be created rather than just moving around what people already have.

Economics explained by cows

FREE ENTERPRISE

- You have two cows.
- You sell one, buy a bull, and build a herd of cows.
- Your herd multiplies, you hire workers and the economy grows.
- You sell the herd and retire on the income.

SOCIALISM

- You work hard and buy two cows.
- Your neighbor doesn't work because the government promised to give him a cow.
- The government takes one of your cows to give to your neighbor.
- You stop working, because what's the use anyway?

COMMUNISM

- You have two cows.
- The government seizes both and provides milk.
- You wait in line for hours to get it.
- It is expensive and sour.

Chapter Three

Discussion Questions

1. Explain the statement, "matter itself is not evil, but the wind behind it is either good or evil depending on how it is used."

2. What are some forms of "wealth"?

3. Why is "creativity" included as wealth?

4. What is "economics"?

5. What form of macroeconomics was in play at the time of Colonial America?

6. Under mercantilism, why was it necessary for nations to have colonies to be prosperous?

7. In your opinion, which system of economics cited in this chapter would encourage human creativity the most? Why?

Chapter 4

TEST BY HISTORY

*H*uman nature does not change. History records actions and events that spring forth from the hearts of men; deeds marked by cruelty, folly, depravity, heroics, and occasionally nobility. Why should it seem surprising that history repeats itself? Let us now consider the history of free enterprise and socialism/communism.

FREE ENTERPRISE

Ancient Israel

The scriptures gave the children of Israel very specific instructions concerning hard work, wealth, conducting business, economics, honesty, responsibility, and charity. Here are several principles found in the Word of God:

- God is your source (Proverbs 8:20-21).

- God owns all wealth (Psalm 24:1).

- Love God not money (Deuteronomy 6:5).

- Give tithes to God (Malachi 3:7-9).

- Be charitable to others. (Leviticus 35:25).

- Work hard (Proverbs 12:14).

- Budget and save (Proverbs 30:25).

- Don't steal (Deuteronomy 5:19).

- Don't covet (Deuteronomy 5:21).

- Prosper (Psalm 35:27).

Monasteries in the Dark and Early Middle Ages

The term "Dark Ages" was not merely a poetic name, but a very apt description of the immense loss Europe suffered when Roman law and order collapsed, giving way to times of great barbarity and uncertainty. As European civilization entered the Dark Ages, an era of intellectual darkness descended which was to last for some eight or nine hundred years. Even the ability to read and write was lost during this time. Only in the monasteries was a faint light of scholasticism kept burning.

> *The term "Dark Ages" was a description of the immense loss Europe suffered when Roman law and order collapsed.*

Catholic monks applied economic principles from the Bible to finance and commerce hundreds of years before the Protestant Reformation and the publication of Adam Smith's book, *The Wealth of Nations*. Although many historians have made the claim that free enterprise, or capitalism, originated in Protestant America, in truth, Catholic monasteries during the Dark and early Middle Ages applied the principles of biblical economics and prospered in a remarkable way.

Although the individual monks took vows of poverty, the monasteries themselves became wealthy. Monasteries were landowners from the beginning, but in the 10th century they began to accumulate substantial amounts of cash, land, and livestock, rivaling the wealthiest aristocrats.

Pilgrims at Plymouth 1620

William Bradford, governor of the little Plymouth colony of Pilgrims, looked to the Bible for God's principles of economics. He studied the scriptures, then applied biblical financial principles based on the Word of God. The seed of free enterprise was sown in Plymouth, and the little colony began to be productive and thrive.

One Nation Under God 1776

The great American experiment of freedom began. *Could man govern himself?* The Declaration of Independence was signed in 1776 by fifty-six patriots who pledged their *lives*, their *fortunes*, and their *sacred honor* for the cause of liberty. As soon as they signed the document, all would be considered guilty of high treason. They were, in effect, signing their own death warrants. But from this courageous act, a new nation of freemen under God was born.

We recognize no sovereign but God, and no king but Jesus!
–John Adams and John Hancock, April 18, 1775.

The Wealth of Nations 1776

Freedom, in and of itself, is grand! However, in 1776 Adam Smith also published *The Wealth of Nations*, which laid out the economic theory of wealth creation. This was the first book of modern economics. The combination of liberty and free enterprise unleashed an explosion of human creativity that catapulted mankind from mule-drawn plows to the moon in 200 years. Human imagination is wonderful but, without finances, ideas are mere dreams rather than reality.

Christian principles

Adam Smith (1723-1790) was a Scottish social philosopher and a pioneer of political economy. Smith argued that healthy self-interest, free markets, and competition produce prosperity. His magnum opus, *The Wealth of Nations*, became one of the most influential works on economics ever written. Smith believed that the creation of wealth must be governed by the Christian guideline of the Golden Rule, to treat others as you would like others to treat you:

> *Do to others whatever you would like them to do to you. This is the essence of all that is taught in the law and the prophets (Matthew 7:12 NLT).*

Healthy self interest benefits individuals and society as a whole.

• Healthy self-interest

Men will gladly work for themselves and their families when they can profit from their own labor. This benefits individuals and society as a whole. Adam Smith wrote:

> It is not from the benevolence of the butcher, the brewer, or the baker that we expect our dinner, but from their regard to their own interest. We address ourselves, not to their

humanity but to their self-love, and never talk to them of our own necessities but of their advantages. Nobody but a beggar chooses to depend chiefly upon the benevolence of his fellow-citizens.[1]

- **Free markets**

A free market operates by the law of supply and demand with limited government interference.

- **The invisible hand**

Smith called competition the *invisible hand*, or force of self-regulation, eliminating the need for outside regulators.

American prosperity

Following the American Revolution, the Founding Fathers designed an economic system based on the principles of free enterprise. The combination of freedom and finance soon made America the most prosperous nation on earth.

> *The combination of freedom and finance made America the most prosperous nation on earth.*

Large middle class

Adam Smith believed "a rising tide lifts all boats."[1] The resultant increase of wealth in America lifted the economy of the whole nation, and created a large middle class. In addition, all individuals had ample opportunity to raise their standing in society through achievement, so there was a general climate of optimism and confidence.

Affluence and generosity

In the American climate of prosperity and Christian values, charity and compassion abounded toward the less fortunate of society. It was widely considered to be a Christian duty to look out for one's fellowman. Affluence bred generosity.

SOCIALISM/COMMUNISM

The folly of intellect

Smart individuals can have foolish ideas! Human *intellect*, man's ability to reason, is not the same as *wisdom*. A man may have a brilliant intellect but still come up with ridiculous conclusions, which produce unwise actions. Thomas Sowell, in his excellent book Intellectuals and Society, explains the difference between intelligence and intellect: intellect is intelligence without judgment and the opposite of wisdom is foolishness.[1]

> *The tree of life was also in the midst of the garden, and the tree of the knowledge of good and evil (Genesis 2:9b).*

> *They did not honor and glorify Him as God. . . But instead they became futile and godless in their thinking [with vain imaginings, foolish reasoning and stupid speculations] and their senseless minds were darkened. Claiming to be wise, they became fools (Romans 1:21-22 AMP).*

INTELLIGENCE = intellect + judgment [1]

INTELLECT - judgment = foolishness

WISDOM = intellect + judgment + God

> *For the LORD gives wisdom; From His mouth come knowledge and understanding; He stores up sound wisdom for the upright (Proverbs 2:6-7).*

> *Go from the presence of a foolish and self-confident man, for you will not find knowledge on his lips. The Wisdom [godly Wisdom, which is comprehensive insight into the ways and purposes of God] of the prudent is to understand his way, but the folly of [self-confident] fools is to deceive (Proverbs 14:7-8 AMP).*

Smart individuals can have foolish ideas!

We can assume that the devil was smart. After all, he was an archangel. But, in his pride, he came up with the ridiculous conclusion that he could actually ascend to the throne of God. It turned out to be a really bad idea!

How you are fallen from heaven,
O Lucifer, son of the morning!
How you are cut down to the ground,
You who weakened the nations!
For you have said in your heart:
'I will ascend into heaven,
I will exalt my throne above the stars of God;
I will also sit on the mount of the congregation
On the farthest sides of the north;
I will ascend above the heights of the clouds,
I will be like the Most High.'
Yet you shall be brought down to Sheol,
To the lowest depths of the Pit (Isaiah 14:12-15).

INTELLECT - judgment = foolishness

Pagan philosophers

Elements of socialism long predated Karl Marx and *The Communist Manifesto* of the late 19th century. The history of socialism can be traced back to Plato's philosophical work, *The Republic,* written around 380 BC. It is considered to be the philosophical "bible of socialism."

Plato (429 BC–347 BC) was a classical Greek philosopher, born in Athens, Greece. In *The Republic,* he suggested that individuals were mere cells within the body politic, and the state should assign their work and responsibilities. Plato felt that the Philosopher class (of which he was one) should rule over the Warrior class, who would protect the state, and the Producer class who would serve the Philosopher class with manual labor, goods, services, and skills.

The Producer class would be denied the benefits of schooling. Plato believed in communal property, as well as the communal sharing of wives. Children would be taken away from their parents and raised in foster homes supervised by the Philosopher class.

Aristotle (384 BC – 322 BC), a student of Plato, criticized Plato's ideas in his work entitled *Politics*, arguing that without private property, no one would assume care of anything. If people had no property, they would be unable to engage in social activities such as hosting guests or doing acts of charity, which encourage community and give meaning to life. Aristotle was wiser than Plato on this subject.

INTELLECT - judgment = foolishness

The Enlightenment (17th -18th centuries)

During the Protestant Reformation, a fresh wind of Christianity swept across Europe. As a result of opposition to Protestantism, many persecuted Christians fled to the American colonies, with a longing for freedom in their hearts. America was destined to be the birthplace of a government of freemen; the twin blessings of freedom in government paired with free enterprise were revealed to the world.

However, every time God moves, the enemy counter-attacks. Socialistic ideas swept through Europe during the French Enlightenment (1650-1800) and even negatively influenced the worldview of many intellectuals in predominately Christian America. However, America's Founding Fathers remained adamantly opposed to socialism.

Alexis de Tocqueville discovered an American nation which was unique in the world. Here, anyone could be a landowner.

Despite ample evidence to the contrary, many American intellectuals studying abroad became enamored with these European ideas that were opposed to everything America stood for. They were so blinded by deception that they failed to comprehend the beauty of what God had created in America.

One *wise* intellectual, the Frenchman Alexis de Tocqueville (1805-1859), came to America and marveled. He was a political thinker and historian, best known today for his two-volume work, *Democracy in America* (1835 and 1840). Tocqueville has been widely cited for his praise of American democracy.

Tocqueville discovered an American nation which was unique in the world. Here, anyone could be a landowner, unlike European nations. He recognized the characteristics that made America great and set it apart from Europe. The goodness of the citizens, the righteousness preached from the pulpits, the Puritan work ethic, the thrift, virtue, charity, and generosity resulted in a prosperous Christian people. He called Americans a brand new breed of man.

Yet, American intellectuals who succumbed to the seduction of the dark, destructive ideas of the Enlightenment were unable to appreciate what was evident right before their eyes.

INTELLECT - judgment = foolishness

Utopian mythology

A utopia is an ideal society or community under a perfectly ordered social, economic, and political system. The word was coined by Sir Thomas More for his 1516 book, *Utopia*. Many philosophers and thinkers have toyed with utopian thought.

Jean-Jacques Rousseau (1712-1778), a Genevan, was a utopian philosopher of the French Enlightenment. His philosophy had a great influence on the French Revolution. Two key concepts that he espoused profoundly impacted both European and American intellectual thought. First, Rousseau believed that man in his primitive state was pure and good, a noble savage. Secondly, civilization corrupted man, so if civilization could be properly constructed, man's innate goodness could come forth. He described this ideal socialist society in his most influential work, *The Social Contract*, published in 1762. The group was everything and the individual was nothing.

> ## *How can individuals possibly be free if they are forced to obey the will of the group?*

Rousseau believed if citizens were *forced to obey* the *general will* of the community, they would become truly free. Question: How can individuals possibly be *free* if they are *forced to obey*, or conform to, the will of the group?

INTELLECT - judgment = foolishness

Utopian socialists

The Industrial Revolution was a chaotic time that wrenched nations from agrarian to industrial societies. Every time great change comes, great adjustment is necessary, but eventually life settles down and society advances. The excesses of poverty and inequality were widely lamented during the upheaval caused by the Industrial Revolution. The first modern socialists were early 19th century Western European social critics in a time of turmoil. During this period, socialism emerged out of a diverse array of doctrines and social experiments associated primarily with British and French thinkers—especially Robert Owen, Charles Fourier, Pierre-Joseph Proudhon, Louis Blanc, and Saint-Simon.

The first use of the word *socialism* is unclear. It has been attributed to a number of people. Regardless of who actually coined the term, Robert Owen, a Welsh manufacturer, is considered the father of the cooperative movement. Robert Owen (1771-1858) was a Welsh manufacturer who sponsored several experimental utopian communities of "Owenites" in England and America, including one at New Harmony, Indiana in 1825.

However, New Harmony soon disintegrated into *disharmony*. The community quickly fell apart, and Owen lamented that the Americans were "too individualistic" to be good socialists. Josiah

Warren, one of the participants, later wrote, "It seemed that the difference of opinion, tastes and purposes increased just in proportion to the demand for conformity" (Periodical Letter II, 1856).[3]

> **The fatal flaw in Marx's philosophy was that it was based in lust for power and love of an ideology — not love for people.**

The socialists tried to answer the dilemmas of the times by looking to their own reasoning for solutions. They did not look to God, but their own intellects.

Professing to be wise, they became fools (2 Thessalonians 3:9-10).

For the wisdom of this world is foolishness with God (1 Corinthians 3:19).

Unfortunately, even the churches in America during 1800-1890 became infected with noble-sounding but impractical ideas of Christian socialism. Many based their attempts at communal living on scriptures such as Acts 4:32, *"they had all things in common."* However, they failed to understand that even good ideas are foolishness without the wisdom, grace, and direct leading of God. Also, scripture must be balanced by scripture, because God directs some individuals to do one thing, and others to do something else entirely.

For even when we were with you, we commanded you this: If anyone will not work, neither shall he eat. For we hear that there are some who walk among you in a disorderly manner, not working at all, but are busybodies (2 Thessalonians 3:9-10).

INTELLECT - judgment = foolishness

Americans were "too individualistic" to be good socialists.

Communism

Karl Marx (1818-1883) was a German philosopher, sociologist, economic historian, journalist, and revolutionary socialist who, along with Friedrich Engels (1820-1825), developed the socio-political theory of Marxism. Marx despised the idea of God. He was an atheist from childhood on. Marx believed that socialism would, in its turn, eventually be replaced by a stateless, classless society called pure communism.

In addition to being fully convinced of the inevitability of socialism and communism, Marx believed in violent revolution to bring it about, arguing that both social theorists and underprivileged people should carry out organized revolutionary action for socio-economic change.

In an interview with the *Chicago Tribune* (January 5, 1879) Marx was asked: "Well, then, to carry out the principles of socialism do its believers advocate assassination and bloodshed?" "No great move-ment has ever been inaugurated without bloodshed," Marx replied. A major shift had occurred. What had once been merely a utopian ideal soon turned deadly.

Fatally flawed

Flawed economic theory: The false assumption of Marx's *economic theory,* described in *Das Kapital*, was his notion that *labor,* the actual *physical handling* of the means, tools, and materials of production was the *source of wealth.*

If this were true, nations with much manual labor and little tech-nology would be more prosperous than those with highly skilled workers and much technology. It is blatantly obvious that this assumption is completely false.

Flawed philosophy: The fatal flaw in Marx's philosophy was that it was based in lust for power and love of an ideology—not love for people. How can you say you to want to *help* people and then *kill* them?

Christianity, on the other hand, is a religion based in love. "God demonstrates His love toward us, in that while we were yet sinners, Christ died for us," (Romans 5:8). Jesus says that the greatest com-mandment is to love God with all your heart, and love your neighbor as you love yourself.

You shall love the Lord your God with all your heart and with all your soul and with all your mind (intellect). This is the great (most important, principal) and first commandment. And a second is like it: You shall love your neighbor as [you do] yourself (Matthew 22:37-40 AMP).

INTELLECT - judgment = foolishness

Early Progressive movement (1890-1920)

Progressivism was a reform movement in America from 1890-1920. Their British counterpart was the Fabian Socialist group. Both groups embraced socialism but saw themselves as elites and looked down on ordinary socialists and communists.

Progressives were not necessarily bad people. Many truly wanted to right the wrongs of society as they saw it. However, "good ideas" rarely lead to good outcomes, especially if they are based on a false premise. Unfortunately for America and mankind, the humanist progressive/socialist/communists planned, organized, and acted to remake the world into their vision. However, it was not God's vision or plan, and was actually antagonistic to God and Christianity.

These intellectuals and social reformers sought to deal with economic, political, and cultural questions that arose during the Industrial Revolution. The Progressives were convinced that these changes signified an end to the old order, the founding principles of the United States, and they were the enlightened ones who must fashion a new order. They strategized and planned to remake America.

Author Upton Sinclair, architect Frank Lloyd Wright, the historian Charles Beard, John Dewey, the father of our modern educational system, and educator Lester Ward were all Progressives working to reshape America. Samuel Gompers in the labor movement, Susan B. Anthony in prohibition, and Jane Adams through social work were progressive activists.

> *Progressives completely reject "the values, beliefs, policies, and practices on which America was founded."*

Political leaders involved in the progressive movement were Woodrow Wilson and Theodore Roosevelt, who sought to undermine the U.S. Constitution itself, and thinkers and strategists such as Herbert Croly and Charles Merriam. Through propaganda and legislation, progressives attempted to recreate American politics, economics, social reforms, and education in a total rejection of the values, beliefs, policies, and practices on which America had been founded.

FOUNDING FATHERS The Grace of Humility	PROGRESSIVES The Sin of Pride
God created man.	Man created god.
Man is a sinner, needs a Savior.	Man is good.
Man is responsible for behavior.	Society makes man bad.
God's Truth is Absolute Truth.	Truth is relative (tolerance).
God gives man rights.	Government gives rights.

The mindset of Progressives:

- **Nature:** Progressive//Socialist/Communist
- **Core belief:** "We are god!"
- **Viewpoint:** "Ordinary people are stupid. We are smart."
- **Tool:** Social engineering
- **Goal:** Remake America (and the world)

Totalitarian poverty

What does history reveal about what is actually created by progressivism/socialism/communism?

- Wealthy ruling class
- Impoverished citizenry

INTELLECT - judgment = foolishness

The Industrial Revolution: spinning history

Sometimes people see what they want to see and ignore the truth. A well-known example is the tale of the Emperor's New Clothes. Tailors said that they were making garments for the king, but only the elite would be able to see them. So when the king was paraded down the street naked, everyone was afraid to say what they really saw. They couldn't admit the truth. Only a child spoke up and said, "But Mother, the emperor has no clothes!"

Improving conditions?

What have you read before about the conditions during the Industrial Revolution? You've probably read history books that portrayed it as a time of great evils. However, honest historians now verify that the alarmists of the day were *not fully accurate* in their assessment of the early Industrial Revolution. Many could not or would not admit Marx's theory was wrong, although the evidence was certainly there. Even during the time of the Industrial Revolution, after the initial upheaval, any objective observer could see that workers were better off.

Incomes began to rise, prices were lower, health conditions and diets improved, housing and working conditions were better.

Industry paid more than agriculture, so wages increased. Life spans were lengthened and child mortality rates decreased, which did increase the numbers of the poor, because previously they would have been dead.

Perhaps the most important development, which proved all of Marx's theories *wrong,* was the emergence of a middle class, which could now afford goods and products previously available only to the wealthy. *The poor didn't get poorer just because the rich got richer.* The standard of living rose dramatically in all levels of society.

Ignoring the facts

One British Marxist, Eduard Bernstein (1850-1932), the chosen successor to Marx and Engels, began to understand the truth.[4] He recorded that the standard of living was actually rising in a positive way even during the early Industrial Revolution. Bernstein observed that, contrary to Marx's beliefs, wages were increasing and prices dropping.

> *During the Industrial Revolution, Eduard Bernstein observed wealth was being created and life was better under capitalism.*

In other words, wealth was being created and life was better under capitalism. This was all the evidence needed to demonstrate the fallacy of Marx's theories in his own lifetime. However, when the cause is more important than facts, the only recourse is willful denial, deception, and outright lies. Despite such convincing evidence to the contrary, ideology was more important to Marx than truth.

INTELLECT - judgment = foolishness

Socialists understand free enterprise leads to *prosperity* and socialism drives nations into *poverty* wherever it is implemented. They don't really believe that socialism benefits people. What they really want is *power*.

Chapter Four
Discussion Questions

1. It has been taught that the free enterprise system began in America. When did free enterprise really begin?

2. What communities of Christians applied free enterprise principles and prospered during the Dark Ages?

3. Adam Smith studied human nature and conditions under which prosperity occurred. Explain Adam Smith's principles and explain how they could benefit individuals and nations:

- Healthy self interest
- Free markets
- The invisible hand

4. What does "a rising tide lifts all boats" mean?

5. What is intellect without judgment? Why?

6. What philosopher is credited with writing the "bible of socialism"?

7. When the Frenchman, Alexis de Tocqueville, came to America, what did he say about Americans?

8. Explain two serious flaws in the economic theory of Karl Marx?

9. What evidence did Marx ignore which proved his ideas wrong while he was still alive?

Chapter 5

TEST BY THE SPIRIT

*M*ammon is material wealth and worldly gain under an evil and corrupt influence, or false god. It is a term also used to describe greed, avarice, and the worship of wealth in biblical literature. Mammon is the opposite of charity.

God and Mammon

In Matthew 6:24, Jesus warned that individuals must make a choice between serving the evil spirit of mammon and the Spirit of God. Whatever or whoever you serve becomes your master.

*No one can serve **two masters**; for either he will hate the one and love the other, or else he will be loyal to the one and despise the other. You cannot serve **God** and **mammon** [emphasis mine] (Matthew 6:24).*

Mammon is not just a concept. There is spiritual energy attached to it. An individual can either serve the spirit of mammon, or use wealth to serve God and lay up treasures in heaven.

Lay up for yourselves treasures in heaven, where neither moth nor rust destroys and where thieves do not break in and steal (Matthew 6:19-20).

Each one's work will become clear; for the Day will declare it, because it will be revealed by fire; and the fire will test each one's work, of what sort it is (1 Corinthians 3:13).

In the beginning, God spoke and the physical universe was created out of tiny particles of energy. Even what we perceive as solid or liquid matter is formed from atoms and molecules, which are made up of energy particles. Atoms and molecules are not evil. Coins and dollar bills are not evil. However, what man does with currency brings it under the authority of either God or Satan.

Money is caught up into a spiritual force like a jet stream.

A flow of purpose

When man uses money, it is *joined to* the purposes of God or the devices of the enemy. Money is caught up into a *spiritual force* like a jet stream. It is conveyed into one kingdom or the other, and it becomes part of a river, or *flow*.

Your riches are corrupted (James 5:2b).

Cornelius, your prayer has been heard, and your alms are remembered in the sight of God (Acts 10:31).

Spirit always has *purpose* attached to it. Purpose has an eventual destination. God is building His kingdom, and the enemy is building his kingdom, which is intended to thwart the will of God and bring destruction to mankind.

*They gave offerings of whatever they could—far more than they could afford!—pleading for the privilege of helping out in the relief of poor Christians. This was totally spontaneous, entirely their own idea, and caught us completely off guard. What explains it was that they had first given themselves unreservedly to God and to us. The other **giving simply flowed out of the purposes of God working in their lives** [emphasis mine] (2 Corinthians 8:4-7 MSG).*

Sowing and reaping

You can sow good seeds or bad seeds, but it always results in a harvest. You can sow finances to God or mammon, but you will reap a harvest.

Whatever a man sows, that he will also reap (Galatians 6:7).

The Spirit of Socialism

Socialism began in the Garden of Eden. It is an economic, social, political, and spiritual system originating from the Tree of the Knowledge of Good and Evil, or humanism. It is not just another idea, opinion, or ideology.

Socialism operates through the sin of greed, and promises something for nothing as the bait. It causes individuals to sin further, breaking the eighth and tenth commandments against stealing and covetousness. As in the parable of the tares in Matthew 13:24-28, the poisonous spirit eventually reveals itself.

Another parable He put forth to them, saying: "The kingdom of heaven is like a man who sowed good seed in his field; but while men slept, his enemy came and sowed tares among the wheat and went his way. But when the grain had sprouted and produced a crop, then the tares also appeared. So the servants of the owner came and said to him, 'Sir, did you not sow good seed in your field? How then does it have tares?' He said to them, 'An enemy has done this.' The servants said to him, 'Do you want us then to go and gather them up?' (Matthew 13:24-28).

Test the spirits!

Test the spirits

The Bible tells us that *we* are responsible to test the spirits. Question the *source* and the *spirit* behind schools of thought, teachings, and philosophies.

Beloved, do not believe every spirit, but test the spirits to see whether they are from God (1 John 4:1).

How do you test the spirits?

Everything that comes from God has His nature attached to it. It has an anointing upon it. It is holy and undefiled. Does it feel pure or sinful, clean or unclean? Is it consistent with the love nature of God? Does it come from the wisdom of God and release the righteousness of God, which is obedience to God's will?

For where envy and self-seeking exist, confusion and every evil thing are there. But the wisdom that is from above is first pure, then peaceable, gentle, willing to yield, full of mercy and good fruits (James 3:16-17).

Free Enterprise	Socialism/Communism
Allows freedom	Denies freedom
Rewards success	Punishes success
Rewards hard work	Rewards laziness
Encourages creativity	Promotes mediocrity
Respects property	Steals property
Promotes charity	Promotes greed
Respects God-given rights	Violates God-given rights
• Life	• Life (abortion, euthanasia)
• Liberty	• Liberty (*political correctness*, control)
• Property	• Property (theft)

THE CHOICE: GOD OR MAMMON

Salvation gives spiritual authority

When you become a citizen of God's kingdom, you have spiritual authority to break the power of mammon over your money and bring it under the Lordship of Christ.

He has delivered us from the power of darkness and CON-VEYED us into the kingdom of the Son of His love [emphasis mine] (Colossians 1:13).

Using money the right way *transfers it* into God's control

Believers have the authority to supernaturally convey money from the spirit of mammon into the kingdom of God—redeeming money from the power of the evil one and bringing it under the authority of the Lord.

We know [positively] that we are of God, and the whole WORLD [around us] is under the POWER [SPIRIT] of the evil one [emphasis mine] (1 John 5:19 AMP).

When an individual gives as an act of worship or godly compassion, anointing is released from the heart. The money is transformed by that accompanying anointing into heavenly riches, or *heavenly treasure* laid up in heaven.

"Will a man rob God?
Yet you have robbed Me!
But you say,
'In what way have we robbed You?'
In tithes and offerings.
You are cursed with a curse,
For you have robbed Me,
Even this whole nation.

Bring all the tithes into the storehouse,

That there may be food in My house,

And try Me now in this,"

Says the Lord of hosts,

"If I will not open for you the windows of heaven

And pour out for you such blessing

That there will not be room enough to receive it (Malachi 3:8-10).

> ### *God calls some individuals to give up*
> ### *wealth and possessions.*

Does God call some individuals to give up wealth and possessions? Yes!

Monks take vows of poverty. Missionaries choose to give up wealth and possessions to serve God. A person who goes into the ministry is, in a sense, foregoing worldly success and wealth to serve God. Traditional churches have often provided parsonages for pastors to compensate for their meager salary.

A religious attitude in some denominations has sometimes caused congregants to view the poverty of the pastor as a mark of holiness. Although this attitude is extreme, a great many Christian ministers do *voluntarily* sacrifice the pursuit of material wealth to serve God. Some ministers prosper financially, of course, but most have a lower standard of living than individuals in the business world or other professions.

Jesus did not give canned answers, but dealt with individuals differently because He knew what was in the heart. In Matthew 19:21-22, the rich young ruler was *ruled* by his wealth. He couldn't let go. Jesus tells the rich young ruler to sell his possessions and give to the poor, but does not tell His friends, Mary and Martha, to give away their house and other possessions.

Jesus answered, "If you want to be perfect, go, sell your posses-sions and give to the poor, and you will have treasure in heaven. Then come, follow me." When the young man heard this, he went away sad, because he had great wealth (Matthew 19:21-22).

Does God call other individuals to finance kingdom business? Yes!

Joseph was given an exalted position, great wealth, and power over all the land of Egypt. God then used Joseph to provide for his own family and the nation of Israel.

And Pharaoh said to Joseph, "See, I have set you over all the land of Egypt." Then Pharaoh took his signet ring off his hand and put it on Joseph's hand; and he clothed him in garments of fine linen and put a gold chain around his neck. And he had him ride in the second chariot which he had; and they cried out before him, "Bow the knee!" So he set him over all the land of Egypt (Genesis 41:41-43).

God calls other individuals to finance kingdom business.

God transferred a tremendous amount of wealth to and through the hands of John Wesley, who was responsible for transforming the nation of England through his program of discipleship, good works, and founding charitable institutions such as hospitals, orphanages, and schools. Because of Wesley, the entire economy of a nation was blessed. Proverbs 13:22 says that God stores up the wealth of the sinner for the righteous:

> *The **wealth** of the **sinner** is stored up for the righteous [emphasis mine].*

The word *righteous* refers to the obedient actions of a person who serves God. A person who is righteous hears what God wants to do and cooperates with God's will. A righteous person co-labors with God as He builds His kingdom on earth.

Property rights

Have you ever been mugged, robbed, or had your residence burglarized? If you yourself have not been a victim, you probably know someone else who was. How does being robbed make a person feel? Almost everyone says they felt *violated*. Why is this? God implanted a sense of right and wrong, theft and personal property, in the heart of man. God gave man the *natural right* to have property to provide for the necessities of life for himself and his family through honest labor.

Fill in the Blanks

What would you call someone who broke into your best friend's apartment and stole their wallet? You would call them a _____.

What if they needed the money to pay their bills? They would still be a _____.

If you stole your friend's money, *you* would be a _____.

If the GOVERNMENT takes YOUR money to pay another individual's bills, or rent, college tuition, student loan, healthcare or give food stamps, the government is a _____.

> *God gave man the natural right to have property to provide for the necessities of life.*

God is your source

The government is not your source. *God* is your source. If you are a Christian, the Bible says to trust God, not man.

It is better to trust in the LORD than to put confidence in man (Psalm 118:8).

• **God commanded the *ravens* to feed Elijah.**

So [Elijah] went and did according to the word of the LORD, for he went and stayed by the Brook Cherith. . . The ravens brought him bread and meat in the morning, and bread and meat in the evening; and he drank from the brook (1 Kings 17:5-6).

• **David declared he had NEVER seen the righteous forsaken by God.**

I have been young, and now am old; Yet I have not seen the righteous forsaken, nor his descendants begging bread (Psalm 37:25).

God promises to provide for you

Your provision comes from God, and He *promises* to care for you. God says that He will provide for you if you will only trust Him! In Matthew 6:25-26, Jesus says that you don't have to worry. Your heavenly Father knows what you need and you are of great value to Him.

Therefore I say to you, do not worry about your life, what you will eat or what you will drink; nor about your body, what you will put on. Is not life more than food and the body more than clothing? Look at the birds of the air, for they neither sow nor reap nor gather into barns; yet your heavenly Father feeds them. Are you not of more value than they? (Matthew 6:25-26)

Nowhere in the Bible does God tell anyone to look to the government to give them the necessities of life. God *warns* against trusting man more than Him. That includes government!

[The Folly of Not Trusting God] Woe to those who go down to Egypt for help,
And rely on horses, Who trust in chariots because they are many,
And in horsemen because they are very strong,
But who do not look to the Holy One of Israel,
Nor seek the Lord! (Isaiah 31:1).

> ### God warns against trusting man more than Him. That includes government!

God says, when you fail to trust Him as your source, your heart has departed from Him. Anything you depend on more than God is an idol, or a false god. If you look to the government to meet your needs, the government has become your god. Who do you really think *cares* more about you anyway? God or the government?

Don't put your life in the hands of experts

who know nothing of life, of salvation life.

Mere humans don't have what it takes;

when they die, their projects die with them.

Instead, get help from the God of Jacob,

put your hope in God and know real blessing!..

He always does what he says—

he defends the wronged,

he feeds the hungry (Psalm 146:3-4 MSG).

They served their idols, which became a snare to them (Psalm 106:36).

Thus says the LORD of hosts: "Return to Me," says the LORD of hosts, "and I will return to you" (Zechariah 1:3)

Government doesn't produce anything

The government doesn't *produce* anything—it only spends. Government doesn't create wealth. It consumes wealth. It gets its money by: (1) taking it from current citizens through taxation, or (2) taking it from future generations by borrowing.

The government uses the income generated by other people: you, your friends, family, and co-workers. Absolutely everything the government gives you comes from real individuals, your neighbors. Disability payments? Neighbors. Food stamps? Neighbors. Medicaid? Neighbors. Unemployment? Neighbors. Many individuals who would feel guilty stealing directly from a friend's wallet, don't hesitate to get all they can from the government. People learn to "work the system" because of:

- Laziness (they don't want to work)
- Greed
- Inability to trust God

> ### *Government doesn't produce anything — it only spends.*

When you trust God, your supply will never run out

Some people sabotage their own provision by failing to give tithes and offerings to God. God promises that when you give to Him, He will pour out blessings for you. If you are faithful in tithes and offerings to demonstrate your trust in God, God assures you that He will provide for you. Whose *promises* do you believe? God's or the government's?

*Will a man rob God? Yet you have robbed Me! But you say, 'In what way have we robbed You?' In tithes and offerings. You are **cursed with a curse**, for you have robbed Me. . . .Bring **all the tithes into the storehouse**, that there may be food in My* *house, and [TEST] Me now in this," says the LORD of hosts, "If I will not open for you the windows of **heaven and POUR OUT for you such blessing that there will not be room enough to receive it.** "And I will **REBUKE THE DEVOURER** for your sakes [emphasis mine] (Malachi 3:8-11 NASB).*

In Malachi 3:9, the word "pour out" in Hebrew, *rûwq*, paints a word picture of God opening a window in heaven and pouring out a flow from a pitcher that never stops flowing. Money is caught up into a *spiritual flow*. God says if you give to Him, He will give to you. The river of blessing will never stop flowing as long as you keep giving. It is a supernatural principle with God's guarantee stamped on it!

The Babylon system

An individual who is physiologically or psychologically dependent on a habit-forming substance is an addict. They become *dependent*. Addicts will even steal money from friends or family members without a qualm. The government makes you dependent on handouts, addicted to the drug of entitlements—which is money they stole from other people.

> *Babylon is a wicked economic system, like a spider's web.*

You become obligated to vote for your caretakers to keep them in power, or your supply will be cut off. You become their slave, trapped by fear. If you have a government job, you are doubly trapped. Babylon is a wicked economic system, like a spider's web. It is an economic system trapping people like a giant evil spider.

It destroys men's souls. Jesus said in Matthew 16:24-26, "What profit is it to a man if he gains the whole world, and loses his own soul? Or what will a man give in exchange for his soul?"

*The **merchants of these things, who became rich by her**, [Babylon] will stand at a distance for fear of her torment [emphasis mine] (Revelation 18:15).*

When an individual worships money, trusting riches instead of God, they are caught in the Babylonian structure. Babylon is an evil world system controlled by the spirit of mammon. Revelation 18:1-9, 23-24 says this:

*After all this I saw another angel come down from heaven with great authority, and the earth grew bright with his splendor. He gave a mighty shout: "**Babylon** is fallen—that great city is fallen! She has become a home for demons. She is a hideout for every foul spirit, a hideout for every foul vulture and every foul and dreadful animal. For all the nations have fallen because of the wine of her passionate immorality. The kings of the world* *have committed adultery with her.* **Because of her desires for extravagant luxury, the merchants of the world have grown rich."**

Then I heard another voice calling from heaven, **"Come away from her, my people. Do not take part in her sins, or you will be punished with her. For her sins are piled as high as heaven, and God remembers her evil deeds.** *⁶* **Do to her as she has done to others. Double her penalty for all her evil deeds. She brewed a cup of terror for others, so brew twice as much for her. She glorified herself and lived in luxury, so match it now with torment and sorrow.**

Therefore, these plagues will overtake her in a single day—death and mourning and famine. She will be completely consumed by fire, for the Lord God who judges her is mighty." And the kings of the world who committed adultery with her and enjoyed her great luxury will mourn for her as they see the smoke rising from her charred remains. . . your merchants were the greatest in the world, and **you deceived the nations with your sorceries. In your streets flowed the blood of the prophets and of God's holy people and the blood of people slaughtered all over the world** *[emphasis mine].*

What does God say about Babylon?

- Babylon is a home (spiritual structure) for demons.
- Governments have committed adultery with her.
- Babylon is an *economic* system.
- God will judge both Babylon and the governments who have sinned with her.
- She is responsible for the slaughter of God's people. (see pages 117-120).

The mark of the beast

The MARK of the BEAST is the *financial* mark of an evil economic system. The mark is on the hand (actions), and forehead (ways of thinking).

*And another angel followed, saying, "**Babylon** is fallen, is fallen, that great city, because she has made all nations drink of the wine of the wrath of her fornication." Then a third angel followed them, saying with a loud voice, "**If anyone worships the beast and his image, and receives his MARK on his forehead or on his hand, he himself shall also drink of the wine of the wrath of God**, which is poured out full strength into the cup of His indignation. He shall be tormented with fire and brimstone* *in the presence of the holy angels and in the presence of the Lamb [emphasis mine] (Revelation 14:8-10).*

TWO KINGDOMS

Clash of kingdoms

God is building His kingdom, but the enemy is building his kingdom, too. Everything that God does is opposed by the enemy. God creates, the devil counterfeits. God creates, the devil destroys. Whenever God initiates something, the enemy designs an evil opposite. God gives life, the devil brings death. God gives prosperity, but the devil gives poverty. The kingdom of God is described as a glorious shining city, and the enemy has a corrupt shadow city. These two spiritual realms are at war for dominance, and humans are the foot soldiers.

God gives prosperity, but the devil gives poverty.

Light and darkness

Light: The Protestant Reformation restored truth to the Church and released the Bible into the hands of the ordinary believers. The old persecutes the new. Christian Protestants were driven out of Europe, and fled for safety to a new land, a safe haven protected by two oceans. They envisioned a nation filled with God's light where men could be free.

The reformation was preceded by the discovery of America, as if the Almighty graciously meant to open a sanctuary to the persecuted in future years, when home should afford neither friendship nor safety.

–Thomas Paine, Common Sense, 1776

Darkness: During the Enlightenment, many turned away from God to worship human reasoning. American intellectuals went to study in Europe, and brought the poisonous seeds of darkness back to America with them. Intelligence can be used for great evil, and the farther away from God, the more evil it will become.

This new world hath been the asylum for the persecuted lovers of civil and religious liberty from every part of Europe. Hither have they fled, not from the tender embraces of the mother, but from the cruelty of the monster; and it is so far true of England, that the same tyranny which drove the first emigrants from home, pursues their descendants still.

–Thomas Paine, Common Sense, 1776

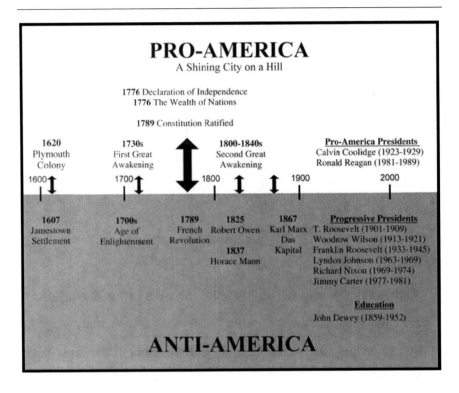

The Conflict Between Light and Darkness

God and greed

God: In the 16th century, God sent missionaries of God's love to North and South America to bring the light of the gospel to the Indians.

Greed: The enemy sent Spanish Conquistadors and other explorers, greedy for gold, who killed and subjugated the Indians.

God: God sent the Plymouth pilgrims to establish a covenantal new land, dedicated to the glory of God. And they were met by

Christian Indians who befriended them. They prospered under God's economic principles of free enterprise. God poured out spiritual refreshings. He continually turned the heart of America back to Himself by sending waves of revival for 200 years, called the First and Second Great Awakenings.

Greed: The enemy sent traders and merchants greedy for wealth to Jamestown. They tried to survive under a form of socialism/communism, many wouldn't work, they stole from the Indians, and most of them died.

Freedom and tyranny

Freedom: The American Revolution was a revolution for the cause of freedom under God. In 1776, a new and free nation was born, the United States of America—based on the principles of Christianity and in covenant with God.

Happily for America, happily, we trust, for the whole human race, they pursued a new and more noble course. They accomplished a revolution which has no parallel in the annals of human society.

–James Madison, Federalist No. 14, November 20, 1787

Tyranny: In 1789 the French Revolution began. The French had already destroyed their own economy by slaughtering the French Huguenots, the Protestants, who made up the nation's middle class—the merchants, businessmen, traders, doctors, and lawyers. Now they had a revolution dedicated to man, not God, and ended up with a Reign of Terror, under the leadership of Maximilien Robespierre. The guillotine became the symbol of the revolutionary cause. Within a year, the French destroyed their own country and brutally murdered an estimated 16,000 to 40,000 people. Will and Ariel Durant wrote in *The Story of Civilization*:

> Most previous revolutions had been against the state or the church, rarely against both at once. . . . Is it any wonder that. . . France went mad. . . . The Philosophers had recognized that, having rejected the theological foundations of morality, they were obligated to find another basis, another system of belief that would incline men to decent behavior as citizens, husbands, wives, parents, and children. But they were not at all confident that the human animal could be controlled without a supernaturally sanctioned moral code. Voltaire and [Jean Jacques] Rousseau finally admitted the moral necessity of popular religious belief.[1]

> ***The American Revolution was a revolution for the cause of freedom under God.***

Lenin, Stalin and Hitler found inspiration for their barbarity in Robespierre. The brutality of the communists and Nazis can be traced back to the deliberate and systematic violence of the French Revolution to crush resistance to the government. The pendulum swung from terror and anarchy to tyranny under a revolutionary dictatorship, and shortly thereafter Napoleon Bonaparte (1769–1821), became emperor from 1804-1815.

Prosperity and poverty

Prosperity: God's principles of economics were also published in the first book of modern economic theory in 1776, Adam Smith's *The Wealth of Nations*. America's Founding Fathers were wise enough to design an economic strategy based on Smith's work. America became a model of prosperity through free enterprise.

Poverty: Every nation that has ever been taken over by communism is impoverished. While it promises prosperity, it always leads to poverty, misery, and tyranny.

Spiritual eyes

All the world sees is the shadow, but those who are God's servants have the *potential* to see the kingdom of God. God calls Christians to look with spiritual eyes and see the kingdom that God is building.

Jesus answered and said to him, "Most assuredly, I say to you, unless one is born again, he cannot see the kingdom of God" (John 3:3).

When the disciples asked Jesus how to pray, He told them to pray that this amazing, glory-filled kingdom of God would be established on earth. And He invites us to participate with Him in the construction of it!

Your kingdom come. Your will be done, on earth as it is in heaven (Matthew 6:10).

Chapter Five
Discussion Questions

1. What makes money good or bad?
2. Does God call some to give away what they have? Why?
3. Does God call others to business and finance? Why?
4. Does the government create wealth? Why or why not?
5. How does government get its money?

6. Compare the clash of good and evil in America in:

- Light and darkness

- God and greed

- Freedom and tyranny

- Prosperity and poverty

Chapter 6

TEST BY THE WORD OF GOD

*G*od wants us to love one another and do good deeds. The Bible encourages us to be charitable, give alms to the poor, and help one another. We are also told we must have the right heart attitude so our giving will be pleasing to God. However, the Bible tells *individual believers* to be generous and compassionate, NOT the civil government. It is not scriptural for civil government to serve as a charitable institution.

> *But don't just listen to God's word. You must do what it says. Otherwise, you are only fooling yourselves. . . . Pure and genuine religion in the sight of God the Father means caring for orphans and widows in their distress and refusing to let the world corrupt you (James 1:22, 27 NLT).*

A devout man and one who feared God with all his household, who gave alms generously to the people, and prayed to God always (Acts 10:2).

So let each one give as he purposes in his heart, not grudgingly or of necessity; for God loves a cheerful giver (2 Corinthians 9:7).

TEST BY THE WORD: SOCIALISM/COMMUNISM

What does the Bible say about socialism/communism?

A thief takes something belonging to someone else, without the owner's permission. The Ten Commandments say that it is wrong to take property owned by another. When the government takes money from citizens by coercion, it is stealing.

You shall not STEAL [emphasis mine] (Deuteronomy 5:19).

God gets even more specific by saying it is a sin to even *think* about wanting what someone else owns. If you *want* something that belongs to someone else, you are sinning. So, when individuals demand the rich be taxed more to give handouts to them, they are coveting the property of others. Socialism breeds sin.

You shall not COVET your neighbor's wife; and you shall not desire your neighbor's house, his field, his male servant, his female servant, his ox, his donkey, or anything that is your neighbor's [emphasis mine] (Deuteronomy 5:21).

• **God, not government, is the source of all provision**

The LORD has blessed my master greatly, and he has become great; and He has given him flocks and herds, silver and gold, male and female servants, and camels and donkeys (Genesis 24:35).

• **Be content with what God gives you**

Let your conduct be without covetousness; be content with such things as you have. *For He Himself has said, "I will never leave you nor forsake you" [emphasis mine] (Hebrews 13:5).*

• **Everyone should work for what he or she gets**

If anyone will not WORK, neither shall he eat [emphasis mine] (2 Thessalonians 3:10).

> *You shall not STEAL. You shall not COVET.*

TEST BY THE WORD: FREE ENTERPRISE

God created wealth

The Bible addresses financial matters more often than prayer, healing, and mercy. God is not against money. He is just against the improper use of it. Seventeen of the thirty-six parables of Jesus are concerned with property and stewardship. Although we may think of wealth in terms of an abundance of material possessions, in the Bible wealth is much more than worldly things. It is the sum total of all that God has provided for us to have a satisfying blessed life while we are here on earth. But it is still His property.

*A river went out of Eden to water the garden, and from there it parted and became four riverheads. The name of the first is Pishon; it is the one which skirts the whole land of Havilah, where there is **gold**. And the gold of that land is good. Bdellium and the onyx stone are there [emphasis mine] (Genesis 2:10-12).*

O LORD, how manifold are Your works! In wisdom You have made them all. The earth is full of Your possessions (Psalm 104:24).

Yours, O LORD, is the greatness, The power and the glory, The victory and the majesty; For all that is in heaven and in earth is Yours; Yours is the kingdom, O LORD, And You are exalted as head over all (1 Chronicles 29:11).

> **God is not against money. He is just against the improper use of it.**

Man is a steward of God's wealth

Wealth is a gift from God. It was created by God and it belongs to God. Everything in the earth, in the ground, above the ground, in the air belongs to God. The cattle on a thousand hills are His, and the gold in every gold mine is owned by God.

*'The **silver** is **Mine**, and the **gold** is **Mine**,' says the LORD of hosts [emphasis mine] (Haggai 2:8).*

The earth is the LORD's, and all its fullness, the world and those who dwell therein (Psalm 24:1).

We are stewards of God's wealth. He is watching what we do with it. He allows us to use what we need to live on, but we are to invest the rest so that it will bring an increase. The following parable from the book of Matthew has often been taught in terms of gifts or special ability, but the word translated *talent* here actually refers to money.

> *It will be like a man going on a journey, who called his servants and entrusted his property to them. To one he gave five talents of money, to another two talents, and to another one talent, each according to his ability. Then he went on his journey.*

> *The man who had received the five talents went at once and put his money to work and gained five more. So also, the one with the two talents gained two more. But the man who had received the one talent went off, dug a hole in the ground and hid his master's money. After a long time the master of those servants returned and settled accounts with them. The man who had received the five talents brought the other five. 'Master,' he said, 'you entrusted me with five talents. See, I have gained five more.' His master replied, "Well done, good and faithful servant! You have been faithful with a few things; I will put you in charge of many things. Come and share your master's happiness!" (Matthew 25:14-30 NIV).*

God ordained *work* for man to gain wealth

The principle of work is found in the book of Genesis. In Genesis 1:1-15, God Himself is working. He created the heavens, the stars and planets, the seas, and everything on earth. God worked for six days and rested on the seventh day. So God was the first to do any work on the earth. Therefore, legitimate work for man reflects the activity of God. Because God is good, work is also good.

> ### *God ordained work for man to gain wealth.*

Also, in Genesis 1:31 (Amplified Bible), God assessed the *quality* of His work. He was satisfied with what He had accomplished, and was pleased with the outcome: "And God saw everything that He had made, and behold, it was very good. . . and He approved it completely." According to this example, it is clear that work should be productive and of high quality.

The Lord God took the man and put him in the garden of Eden to WORK it and keep it [emphasis mine] (Genesis 2:15).

Blessed is everyone who fears the LORD, who walks in His ways. When you eat the labor of your hands, you shall be happy, and it shall be well with you (Psalm 128:1-2).

God praises a good work ethic

Lazy hands make a man poor, but diligent hands bring wealth (Proverbs 10:4 NIV1984)

Go to the ant, you sluggard! Consider her ways and be wise, which, having no captain, overseer or ruler, provides her supplies in the summer, and gathers her food in the harvest (Proverbs 6:6-11).

A good man makes a profit

God does not want man to *love* money, but He does want him to be blessed and prosperous. Proverbs 13:22 says a good man should profit so much from his labor that he leaves an inheritance sizeable enough to pass on to both his children and grandchildren.

In all labor there is PROFIT [emphasis mine] (Proverbs 14:23a).

A GOOD man leaves an inheritance to his children's children, but the sinner's wealth is laid up for the righteous [emphasis mine] (Proverbs 13:22).

*Beloved, I pray that you may **prosper** [PROFIT] in all things and be in **health**, just as your soul **prospers** [emphasis mine] (3 John 1:2).*

Whether or not you realize it, many individuals in the Bible had great wealth. We are told that Abram was "extremely rich" in Genesis 13:2. Jacob was "very wealthy" (Genesis 30:43), and Isaac became a very rich man and scripture tells us that "his wealth continued to grow" (Genesis 26:13).

In Genesis 13:2, the Bible says King David had incredible wealth, and in 1 Chronicles 29:3, we learn that he was able to give all the gold and silver for the building of the Temple, an enormous amount in today's terms. The Queen of Sheba visited King Solomon and was left breathless when she saw the extent of his wealth. God also demonstrated He had no difficulty getting wealth into the hands of faithful stewards to accomplish His purposes.

> ### *According to the Bible, a good man makes a profit.*

God has a plan to fill the earth with His glory

When man sinned, he lost the covering of God's glory. Since that time, God has wanted His glory to be released on earth again.

Truly, as I live, all the earth shall be filled with the glory of the LORD (Numbers 14:21).

It takes money to fill the earth with God's glory

Any poor man can preach the gospel but it takes wealth to transform a nation. Although God wants to bless us personally, money has a mission, and God is looking for willing partners to complete this mission. John Wesley wrote in one of his sermons, "When the possessor of Heaven and Earth brought you into being and placed you in this world, He placed you here not as an owner but as a steward. As such, He entrusted you for a season with goods of various kinds. But the sole property of these still rests in Him nor can ever be alienated from Him, as you are not your own but His. Such as likewise all you enjoy."[1]

John Wesley was such a faithful steward the entire nation of England was transformed through his faithful use of finances and Christian discipleship. Lavish amounts of money were contributed to him and the work he was doing, but that wealth was channeled into schools, orphanages, hospitals, and many other charitable institutions and good deeds, and Wesley himself died with few worldly goods of his own. Everything that God brought to Wesley was given back to establish the work of the Lord on earth.

The Spirit of God is the Spirit of the Creator

God gives man *power* to get wealth. In Deuteronomy 8:18, the word "power" in the original Hebrew is *koach*, which means *to create together, to produce, to industrialize* to get wealth. God is a Creator. His Spirit is a *creating* spirit. Man has been given the privilege to co-labor with God in creation by receiving revelation for wealth creation.

And you shall remember the LORD your God, for it is He who gives you POWER [Hb. Koach: to create together, to produce, to industrialize] to get WEALTH, that He may establish His COVENANT [emphasis mine] (Deuteronomy 8:18).

By which have been given to us exceedingly great and precious promises, that through these you may be partakers of the divine nature (2 Peter 1:4).

For we have become partakers of Christ (Hebrews 3:14).

> **Any poor man can preach the gospel but it takes wealth to transform a nation.**

God prospers His servants to establish His covenant

What is God's ultimate purpose for wealth? To advance the kingdom of God on earth. And that takes money! He blesses mankind with God-given ability to get wealth so that, by using this money, God can bring the nations of the earth into covenant with Him (Deuteronomy 8:18).

*The LORD be magnified, Who delights in the **prosperity** of His servant [emphasis mine] (Psalm 35:27 NASB).*

Therefore thus says the LORD: "I am returning to Jerusalem with mercy; My house shall be built in it," says the LORD of hosts, "And a surveyor's line shall be stretched out over Jerusalem. Again proclaim, saying, Thus says the LORD of hosts: "My cities shall again spread out through PROSPERITY; The LORD will again comfort Zion, and will again choose Jerusalem." [emphasis mine] (Zechariah 1:16-17).

God owns the whole world

We do not really own anything except what is lent to us by God. We are stewards of what belongs to Him. In Psalm 50:12, God says, " If I were hungry, I would not tell you; For the world is Mine, and all its fullness."

The earth is the Lord's, and all its fullness,
The world and those who dwell therein.
For He has founded it upon the seas,
And established it upon the waters (Psalm 24:1-2).

God gives property to people

Scripture teaches the importance of private property. Psalm 115:16 says, "The heaven, even the heavens, are the LORD's; But the earth He has **given** to the **children of men**." Although earth belongs to God, God gives man the right to have a portion of His property to provide the necessities of life. If something is *given* to you, it is your *private property*. You own it. If anyone takes your property from you, they have committed a crime. God says it is sin to steal someone's property. Property and property rights are important to God.

Every three-year-old child knows the concept of "mine," and objects if another child takes his or her toy. Although you may teach children they should share, you assure them that the toy will be returned. You also teach them, when they give a birthday gift to a friend, the gift becomes the friend's *property*.

- God gives property and land for man to use.
- *Then the LORD appeared to Abram and said, "To your descendants I will give this land" (Genesis 12:7).*
- The 8th Commandment, *"You shall not steal,"* reveals that God considers private property to be important. God forbids stealing what belongs to another person.
- The 10th Commandment, *"You shall not covet,"* command us to not even THINK about stealing property belonging to another person.

There are many forms of stealing

- Scripture mandates that all measurements and standards should be accurate, consistent, and unchanging, to prevent the cheating of customers (Leviticus 19:35-36).
- The Bible forbids cheating or defrauding others (Leviticus 19:13).

- The Bible prohibits moving markers that define the boundaries of one's land and also forbids lying (Deuteronomy 19:14-20).

Free enterprise: Property is protected
Socialism/communism: Property is plundered

Property is the foundation for the rule of law

Why must government protect rights? Because God gave man the basic human rights of life, liberty, and private property. These are *rights given to man by God Himself*. The **Bill of Rights** was a written guarantee that rights of American citizens would not be violated. By the way, the Bill of Rights was designed to limit *governmental reach* into the lives of private citizens. It was never intended to be used against individuals.

- The Declaration of Independence specifies *property rights* ("the pursuit of happiness") as a right given to man by God Himself.

- Protection of these rights is the *purpose* for government.

God gives man the right to life and the right to own the property necessary to sustain life for himself and his family. Man pays his own "time and effort and ingenuity," the currency of life, to earn property, so it is his right to keep what he has purchased with part of his life. It is wrong for another individual or government to take his property by coercion or force.

- A person "pays" his time and labor (the currency of life) to purchase property.

What was happening in the American colonies concerning property prior to the Revolutionary War? The British were engaging in arbitrary seizure of people's property and levying excessive taxes, fines, duties and tariffs. Imagine what it would be like if you no longer had any right to own, keep, or protect anything you now have. The neighbor, the looter, or the government could take whatever they wished and you would have no recourse.

> *"We cannot be free without being secure in our property."*

Noah Webster defined property as "the exclusive right of possessing, enjoying and disposing of a thing; ownership." In the beginning, the Creator gave man dominion over the earth, over the fish of the sea and the fowls of the air, and over every living thing. This is the foundation of man's property in the earth and in all its productions. Prior occupancy of land and of wild animals gives to the possessor the property of them. The labor of inventing, making or producing anything constitutes one of the highest and most indefeasible titles to property."[2]

John Dickinson, signer of the Constitution, wrote, "Let these truths be indelibly impressed on our minds: (1) that we cannot be happy without being free; (2) that we cannot be free without being secure in our property; (3) that we cannot be secure in our property if without our consent others may as by right take it away."[3]

But if anyone does not provide for his own, and especially for those of his household, he has denied the faith and is worse than an unbeliever (1 Timothy 5:8).

A good man leaves an inheritance to his children's children (Proverbs 13:22a).

- If an individual steals property it is a crime.
- If a government steals property it is a crime.

You who preach that a man should not steal, do you steal? (Romans 2:21b).

- If it is morally wrong for an individual, it is morally wrong for a government.
- Socialism/communism is LEGALIZED THEFT.
- Socialism makes SIN lawful.
- The law itself becomes an IMMORAL instrument of theft.

Socialism is anti-Christ:

- Socialism attacks the philosophy of Christians and Jews.
- Socialism teaches that all Bible-believers are enemies of socialism. (They are right!)
- Socialism crushes creativity (Spirit of Creation).

Socialism is morally wrong because it:

- Teaches it is wrong to prosper and profit.
- Steals from some to give to others.
- Extinguishes personal motivation and incentive.
- Destroys the individual work ethic.
- Makes sin legal.

God emphasizes the *moral excellence* of free enterprise. He praises the *virtuous* woman for hard work, diligence, doing business, and making a profit.

She also rises while it is yet night, and provides food for her household, and a portion for her maidservants. She considers a field and buys it; from her profits she plants a vineyard (Proverbs 31:15-16).

The prosperity of Israel

The Israel of Jesus' day was still a land of "milk and honey" with fertile farmlands,[4] grassy hills "clothed with flocks," and rivers teeming with fish. Literature and archaeological finds substantiate that it was wealthy in forests, abundant in all types of natural resources, and exporter of fruit, wine, olives, grain, spices and oils.[5] It was one of the prize possessions held by the Roman empire!

> ### The Israel of Jesus' day was still a land of "milk and honey."

The towns and cities in the time of Jesus were known for the finest examples of engineering and architecture. Sepphoris, three miles from Nazareth, "had all the trappings of a modern, wealthy city of the Roman Empire. It boasted an elaborate water system with a cistern a thousand feet long."[6] Homes of the day were not all minimal dirt floor dwellings, as often depicted in Sunday school pictures, although there *were* simple peasant houses, especially in rural areas.

For the most affluent Israelites, city dwellings were often multiple story dwellings with courtyards and beautiful architectural stonework and details. Houses were constructed with columns, atriums, interior courtyards, and mosaics, often with Roman influence, and commonly plastered inside and out with lime plaster.[7] We know that, prior to the day of Pentecost, the disciples waited together in an upper room of a house in Jerusalem which was large enough to hold 120 individuals.

> *Then they returned to Jerusalem from the mount called Olivet, which is near Jerusalem, a Sabbath day's journey. And when they had entered, they went up into the upper room where they were staying: Peter, James, John, and Andrew; Philip and Thomas; Bartholomew and Matthew; James the son of Alphaeus and Simon the Zealot; and Judas the son of James. These all continued with one accord in prayer and supplication, with the women and Mary the mother of Jesus, and with His brothers. . . altogether the number of names was about a hundred and twenty (Acts 1:12-15).*

Israel was also the "crossroads of the ancient world." The main trade route of the civilized world, the Via Maris, passed through it. One of the finest examples of the skill used in city building was found in Caesarea. Caesarea was built into one of the most renowned seaports of its day, with a forty-acre natural harbor, complete with a lighthouse to guide ships. "Much of the city was built with imported marble and the city had an elaborate sewer system that was cleansed by the sea."[8]

Israel was the "crossroads of the ancient world." The main trade route of the civilized world, the Via Maris, passed through it.

Over the centuries following the destruction of Jerusalem, Israel was de-forested and ruined. This resulted in soil erosion in large areas. It was also a common custom for conquering armies to sow the land with salt to destroy the soil. "The Turks dealt the final blow in the period of the first world war, when they cut down the last remnants of the forests to keep the railways running!"[9]

I will bring the land to desolation, and your enemies who dwell in it shall be astonished at it. I will scatter you among the nations and draw out a sword after you; your land shall be desolate and your cities waste (Leviticus 26:32-33).

The land of Israel stayed in this sad state until the return of the Jews to the land following World War I. They began the arduous task of the modern day reclamation of the land. It was no small task, but once more it can be said:

> *The wilderness and the wasteland shall be glad for them, And the desert shall rejoice and blossom as the rose; It shall blossom abundantly and rejoice, Even with joy and singing. The glory of Lebanon shall be given to it, The excellence of Carmel and Sharon (Isaiah 35:1-2).*

Jesus, the capitalist

When Joseph and Mary journeyed to Bethlehem to pay taxes before the birth of Jesus, they weren't homeless or destitute. If they had to pay taxes, they had money. Although they had planned to stay in an inn, there was no vacancy because Bethlehem was flooded with travelers on the same mission.

Joseph was a small business owner.

Joseph, the earthly father of Jesus, may not have been just a maker of simple, wooden furniture, as he has often been portrayed. In the Gospels, the word *tekton* is used to describe Joseph (Matthew 13:55; cf., Mark 6:3). A *tekton*, "a carpenter who builds," was not just an ordinary carpenter, but more like a general contractor, described by Paul in 1 Corinthians 3:10 as a "wise master builder."[7] Rocks and cut stone were the main building materials of the day, rather than wood, so a *tekton* would work as a stonemason, often using local limestone and imported marble.[10] However, even if Joseph did just make furniture, he was still a small business owner.

Hebrew families often lived in family housing complexes called *insulae* (singular *insula*) designed for a multi-generational extended family, constructed around an open courtyard. The insula is referenced in the New Testament as "household," meaning "an extended family living together."[11] It is possible Jesus, and perhaps His brothers, worked alongside Joseph to construct their own family home.

"Where did this Man [Jesus] get this wisdom and these mighty works? Is this not the carpenter's [Gk. tekton] son? Is not His mother called Mary? And His brothers James, Joses, Simon, and Judas? And His sisters, are they not all with us? Where then did this Man get all these things?" So they were offended at Him (Matthew 13:54-57).

Contrary to popular mythology, therefore, it is unlikely Jesus was a poor man. Even if the family weren't wealthy, they were almost certainly comfortably middle class. It is not stated in the Bible, but Joseph and his sons would surely have hired other workers, craftsmen, and artisans during construction, as was the common practice at that time. The eldest son was expected to take over the family business someday, so Jesus would have learned skills for building as well as good business practices from Joseph.

When Jesus taught the parable of the "house built on a rock," He understood the importance of building on a proper foundation from experience. Jesus also called Himself the *Cornerstone* and said He is the *builder* of His church, using *living stones* as the building material.

Therefore everyone who hears these words of mine and puts them into practice is like a wise man who built his house on the rock. The rain came down, the streams rose, and the winds blew and beat against that house; yet it did not fall, because it had its foundation on the rock. (Matthew 7:24 NIV).

The stone which the builders rejected
Has become the chief cornerstone (Matthew 21:42).
[O]n this rock I will build My church (Matthew 16:17).

Jesus Christ Himself being the chief cornerstone, in whom the whole building, being fitted together, grows into a holy temple in the Lord, in whom you also are being built together for a dwelling place of God in the Spirit (Ephesians 4:19-22).

Coming to Him as to a living stone, rejected indeed by men, but chosen by God and precious, you also, as living stones, are being built up a spiritual house (1 Peter 4:2).

In the Parable of the Minas, Luke 19:11-26, Jesus praises those who buy, sell, and trade. He tells the parable of a master who gives each one a certain amount of money and commands them to "do business." Jesus encourages his disciples to become good entrepreneurs. Jesus was a *capitalist*.

Jesus encourages his disciples to become good entrepreneurs.

• **The master provides servants with money**

The master provides them with some of his own property, giving each a *mina*. How much was a mina worth? One mina was roughly the value of twenty years work by an ordinary person. He entrusted them with a lot of money!

• **The servants are expected to do business**

The ten servants are clearly expected to do business with this money. Therefore, the master has confidence that they have both ability and opportunity. Jesus tells his disciples the parable in Luke 19:11-26:

*Now as they heard these things, [Jesus] spoke another parable, because He was near Jerusalem and because they thought the kingdom of God would appear immediately. Therefore He said: "A certain nobleman went into a far country to receive for himself a kingdom and to return. So he called **ten of his servants**, delivered to them **ten minas**, and said to them, '**Do business** till I come' [emphasis mine].*

• The master asks for an accounting

When the master returns after a long absence, he asks his servants to give an accounting. He checks out their ledger sheets, and calculates how well they had done. The master wants to know just how much they had increased the initial investment.

And so it was that when he returned, having received the kingdom, he then commanded these servants, to whom he had given the money, to be called to him, that he might know how much every man had gained by trading (Luke 19:15).

• The first servant is praised and rewarded

The first servant is praised by the master. Of all the servants, this is the only one to whom the master say "well done" and calls him "faithful." Then the master gives the servant a significant reward for his faithfulness, "have authority over ten cities."

> *Then came the first, saying, 'Master, your mina has earned ten minas.'* [17] *And he said to him, 'Well done, good servant; because you were faithful in a very little, have authority over ten cities' (Luke 19:16).*

The master asks his servants to give an accounting.

• The next servant is only rewarded

The next servant receives a reward of authority over five cities, but the master does not tell him "well done." He receives a reward but is not praised.

> *And the second came, saying, 'Master, your mina has earned five minas.' Likewise he said to him, 'You also be over five cities' (Luke 19:18-19).*

• The last servant is reprimanded

Another servant comes to the master, but he comes with an excuse. The servant accurately states that the master is an austere man, because the master agrees with this assessment. The word *austere* means "demanding hard work and diligent carefulness." The last servant confesses that he didn't even try his hand with business, but put his mina in storage.

> *Then another came, saying, 'Master, here is your mina, which I have kept put away in a handkerchief. For I feared you, because you are an austere man [demanding hard work and diligent carefulness]. You collect what you did not deposit, and reap what you did not sow' (Luke 19:20-21).*

This servant is reprimanded for being lazy and nonproductive. The master calls him *wicked*. He neither engaged in hard work nor was he diligent. Was there no one who could advise him, no one who could mentor him in business and investing? He certainly could have asked the other servants to give him some financial advice!

> *And he said to him, 'Out of your own mouth I will judge you, you wicked servant. You knew that I was an austere man, collecting what I did not deposit and reaping what I did not sow. Why then did you not put my money in the bank, that at my coming I might have collected it with interest?' (Luke 19:22-23).*

- ## The master is not a *socialist*

What does the master do? The master obviously isn't a socialist. He doesn't make the other servants give some of their money to the lazy servant. Rather, he says take the servant's mina from him, give it to the servant with ten minas, and leave the wicked servant with nothing at all!

- ## "From those who do nothing, even what little they have will be taken away."

The master does not take from the *haves* to give to the *have-not*. He is not a Robin Hood, taking from the rich to give to the poor. Instead, the master takes the mina from the have-not and gives it to the one who prospered the most. He increases the reward of the most hard-working and diligent servant. God clearly expects us to be good stewards of the wealth He has given us.

> *And he said to those who stood by, 'Take the mina from him, and give it to him who has ten minas.' (But they said to him, 'Master, he has ten minas.') For I say to you, that to everyone who has will be given; and from him who does not have, even what he has will be taken away from him.'*
> *"'Yes,' the [master] replied, 'and **to those who use well what they are given, even more will be given. But from those who***

do nothing, even what little they have will be taken away'
[emphasis mine] (Luke 19:24-26 NLT).

> ### *The master takes from the have-not and gives it to the one who prospered the most.*

TEST BY THE WORD:
CHARITY AND THE POOR

"You have the poor with you always"

Jesus Himself tells us that there will always be some people who are poor. Life is not fair. Some people have more potential than others. The Declaration of Independence says that all men are created equal before God, and that all should have equal opportunity for life, liberty, and pursuit of happiness. But there is no guarantee of equal outcomes, equal talent, or equal wealth.

For you have the poor with you always, and whenever you wish you may do them good (Mark 14:7).

So what, then, does the Bible say to do about the *poor?* To help them, of course. But God also tells us *how.* He has provided us with an opportunity to sow good deeds, care for our fellowman, and lay up *for ourselves treasure in heaven through acts of charity.*

Do not neglect to do good and to share what you have, for such sacrifices are pleasing to God (Hebrews 13:16)

Blessed are those who are generous, because they feed the poor (Proverbs 22:9).

Lay up for yourselves treasures in heaven, where neither moth nor rust destroys and where thieves do not break in and steal (Matthew 6:20).

What is *charity?* Charity is *voluntary* provision of help or relief to the poor based on benevolence, goodwill, and love of one's fellowman. Charity is a matter of the heart. Only individuals can do charity, because charity requires genuine love or it is worthless in the eyes of God.

*And **though I bestow all my goods to feed the poor. . .but have not love**, it profits me nothing [emphasis mine] (Corinthians 13:3).*

If this is the case, the government *cannot* do true charity. It is actually unconstitutional for the government to redistribute the wealth of U.S. citizens to benefit one group of people more than another group. Do you really think most politicians genuinely care about people—or do they just want to fund their pet projects, get your vote, and stay in power? The federal government wants to *control the* people and *force* you to give them your money. (By the way, liberal politicians give almost nothing to charity out of their *own* pockets!)

Each one must give as he has decided in his heart, not reluctantly or under COMPULSION, for God loves a cheerful giver [emphasis mine] (2 Corinthians 9:7).

What the Founders said about socialism

The moment the idea is admitted into society that property is not as sacred as the laws of God, and that there is not a force of law and public justice to protect it, anarchy and tyranny commence. If 'Thou shalt not covet' and 'Thou shalt not steal' were not commandments of Heaven, they must be made inviolable precepts in every society before it can be civilized or made free.

–John Adams, A Defense of the Constitutions
of Government of the United States of America, 1787

I am for doing good to the poor, but I differ in opinion of the means. I think the best way of doing good to the poor, is not making them easy in poverty, but leading or driving them out of it.

–Benjamin Franklin, The London Chronicle,
November 29, 1766

A wise and frugal government. . .shall restrain men from injuring one another, shall leave them otherwise free to regulate their own pursuits of industry and improvement, and shall not take from the mouth of labor the bread it has earned. This is the sum of good government.

–Thomas Jefferson, First Inaugural Address,

March 4, 1801

If we can prevent the government from wasting the labors of the people, under the pretence of taking care of them, they must become happy.

–Thomas Jefferson, letter to Thomas Cooper,

November 29, 1802

Persons and property are the two great subjects on which Governments are to act; and that the rights of persons, and the rights of property, are the objects, for the protection of which Government was instituted. These rights cannot well be separated.

–James Madison, Speech at the Virginia

Convention, December 2, 1829

Chapter Six
Discussion Questions

1. What does the Bible say about socialism/communism?

2. Who created and owns wealth?

3. What does that make man in regard to wealth?

4. What means did God ordain for man to get wealth? Why?

5. What does it take to fill the earth with God's glory? Why?

6. What divine attribute did God give to man so he could get wealth?

7. What is the foundation for the rule of law? Why?

8. Socialism causes what two sins?

9. Socialism is anti-Christ because:

   •

   •

   •

10. Joseph, the husband of Mary, was a *tekton*. What does that mean?

11. In what way was Jesus an *entrepreneur*?

12. Who does the master praise in the parable of the minas?

13. Who does the master take from to reward another?

14. What did the faithful servant do that brought such a reward?

15. Was Jesus a socialist?

Chapter 7

TEST BY THE FRUIT

However beautiful the strategy, you should occasionally look at the results.

−Winston Churchill

Whenever you want to determine the probable outcome of something, it is wise to consider the *source*. Jesus tells us that we can discern the *nature* of the source by becoming fruit inspectors. A good tree bears good fruit. A bad tree bears bad fruit.

You will know them by their fruits. . . . A good tree cannot bear bad fruit, nor can a bad tree bear good fruit (Matthew 7:16-19).

Fruit of free enterprise: The source of free enterprise is the Word of God and the Spirit of God. The fruit of free enterprise is always **prosperity**.

Fruit of socialism: The source of socialism is human reasoning and spirit of humanism (evil). The fruit of socialism (and communism) is **poverty and misery**.

> **A good tree bears good fruit.**
> **A bad tree bears bad fruit.**

THE STANDARD OF LIVING FRUIT

Free enterprise directly increases per capita income, raising the standard of living wherever it is practiced. A free society significantly decreases poverty and increases prosperity across the board for the entire population. When there is limited government interference, free enterprise allows people to determine their own standard of living, based on aptitude, perseverance, and work ethic.

In a free enterprise economy, people believe they can improve their standard of living by hard work. When the standard of living improves for individuals, the economy of the nation improves. Free enterprise creates a large middle class with mobility between the levels of society. Poor individuals are able to lift themselves out of poverty, and members of the middle class can become wealthy.

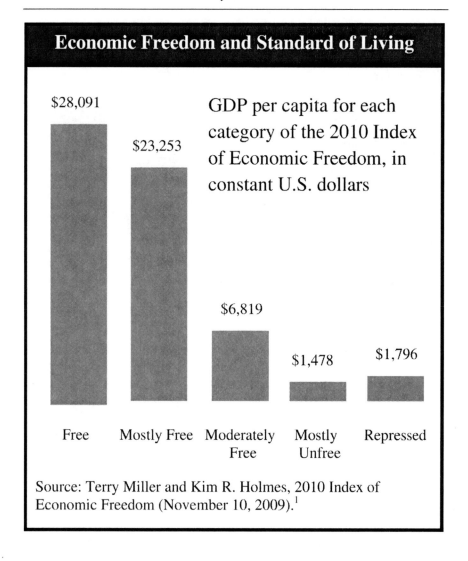

Economic Freedom and Standard of Living

$28,091

$23,253

GDP per capita for each category of the 2010 Index of Economic Freedom, in constant U.S. dollars

$6,819

$1,478

$1,796

Free   Mostly Free   Moderately Free   Mostly Unfree   Repressed

Source: Terry Miller and Kim R. Holmes, 2010 Index of Economic Freedom (November 10, 2009).[1]

THE CREATIVITY FRUIT

The necessary ingredients for creativity are an atmosphere that (1) rewards success and hard work, (2) allows competition for excellence, and (3) celebrates individualism. When people have a reason to dream with a reasonable possibility of achievement, human creativity is unleashed. If people feel like there is no chance to succeed, they stop trying.

Free Enterprise	Socialism
Rewards success	Punishes success
Rewards hard work	Rewards laziness
Promotes excellence	Promotes mediocrity
Encourages individual creativity	Encourages group conformity
Private property protected	Private property plundered
Individual rights protected	Individual rights violated
Limited government regulation	Much government regulation

Individual Creativity

- **Free enterprise rewards creativity** by rewarding success and hard work, promoting excellence, encouraging individual creativity, protecting both property rights and individual rights, and having limited governmental regulation.

Group Conformity

- **Socialism crushes creativity** by punishing success, rewarding laziness, promoting mediocrity and group conformity, violating property and individual rights, and having burdensome government regulation.

Have you heard the oft repeated myth that we are using up the planet's valuable natural resources and the world is facing a crisis? This has been preached so often most people probably believe it. One day this absurdity will be exposed as a fraud, just like the global warming hoax. *The Ultimate Resource 2,* by Julian Simon, reveals the truth. If you are curious and read the book, you would completely reset your thinking.[2]

Of course, God has given us the responsibility to be good stewards of His property, planet earth. That is not the point. Certainly it is wrong to set forest fires and pollute lakes and rivers. It is wrong to be wasteful and destructive. However, the alarmists are not being truthful. For example, one film[3] being shown in elementary school classrooms tells children, "In the United States, we have less than 4 percent of our original forests left." However, according to the U.S. Forest service, 33 percent of America is forested and has been stable for one hundred years! The film also states, "The USA is 5 percent of global population, but uses 30 percent of resources." This is true, but very misleading. The United States also produces almost 30 percent of the world's GDP. This demonstrates we are *remarkably efficient*, not wasteful!

> *Without human creativity, there are no resources. The human spirit is the ultimate resource!*

The truth of the matter is that every material classified today as a natural resource was once considered useless or even a downright nuisance. Only human creativity could make apparently worthless materials marketable and beneficial. Without human creativity, there are no resources. The *human spirit* is the ultimate resource!

Crude oil became a resource only when someone first creatively figured out that it can be used to satisfy human wants. And even then our ability to use it became a reality only because many other people creatively devised each of the various tools and processes necessary for extracting and refining crude oil. . . . Anything that hampers human creativity is thus a curse to all humankind. Anything that encourages human creativity is a boon.[4]

Freedom to create coupled with free enterprise to finance dreams are the necessary ingredients to take what most people would consider impractical or impossible and turn one generation's daydreams into the next generation's necessities.

> *Every material classified today as a natural resource was once considered useless or even a downright nuisance.*

THE PROSPERITY FRUIT

History has demonstrated that the fruit of free enterprise is **prosperity**. The fruit of socialism/communism is always **poverty and misery**. For example, the American Indian tribes who receive the most government "help" live as wards of the state, many with a poverty rate of 25 percent. However, the Lumbee tribe of Robeson

County, North Carolina, is not eligible for the help other tribes receive because the government does not recognize them as sovereign.

The Lumbees start their own businesses, own their own homes, and most do not desire handouts. They are self-sufficient, industrious, and very prosperous capitalists. A Lumbee businessman, Ben Chavis, commented that the Indians on the reservation do so poorly because they "have been trained to be communists."[5]

Socialism divides "the pie"

Socialism says that there is a fixed amount of wealth that must be redistributed. When you believe there is only one pie, how can it be divided up equally so everyone can have a "fair share"? This concept stirs up envy toward those who have a bigger "piece of the pie." Redistribution of wealth requires coercive taking from those with "bigger pieces" to give to others who have less. Unfortunately, the more times the pie is divided, the smaller the pieces become.

Capitalism makes *more* pies

Free enterprise, on the other hand, offers a much better solution. Rather than re-dividing the pie into smaller and smaller pieces. . .free enterprise *makes more pies!* Free enterprise is the *only* system that actually creates *more* wealth instead of just shifting around what people already have.

SOCIALISM: Divide the Pie

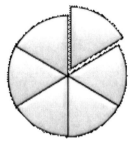

CAPITALISM: Make More Pies

SOCIALISM/COMMUNISM POPERTY FRUIT

Jamestown

In June of 1606, King James I granted a charter to a group of London entrepreneurs, the Virginia Company (later The London Company), to plant a settlement at Jamestown, Virginia. In 1607, the London Company sent a group of businessmen to set up a colony in Virginia. The settlers were told to follow these rules of communal living:

- No private property
- Communal living
- Leader assigns tasks

They took no women and only one clergyman. Many of the men who went were British gentlemen who refused to work because they considered work to be beneath their station in life. The first group totally perished. More settlers were sent but, needless to say, they also fared very poorly. Although they attempted a cover-up, eventually the truth leaked out and reports made it back to Europe.

Communism was unsuccessful in the Jamestown settlement.

Plymouth

The same London Company decided to try the strategy again with these same rules with the Pilgrims. Surely Christians in the Plymouth Colony would be able to succeed at communal living more easily than the Jamestown settlers. The settlers were told to follow these same rules of communal living:

- No private property
- Communal living
- Leader assigns tasks

Unfortunately, nearly half of the settlement starved the first winter. People complained about their assigned tasks, some claimed exemption due to disabilities, and Governor William Bradford also noticed that those who worked the least showed up with the biggest baskets to collect their share of the food.

***Christian communism* was unsuccessful in the Plymouth colony!**

> ***Those who worked the least showed up with the biggest baskets to collect food.***

Bradford then went to the Bible and came up with a new plan based on God's principles of prosperity. This changed the entire economic system of the colony.

- Each family was given their own land to work.
- Families must provide for themselves.
- Anything they produced was their own property.
- If they didn't work, then they had nothing to eat.

The transformation was astounding. Everyone went into the fields willingly and worked diligently. They later held a thanksgiving feast to celebrate the great bounty and to bless God for His biblical principles of FREE ENTERPRISE.

The Plymouth colony thrived under the free enterprise system as the basis for a successful economic policy. These same principles eventually made America the wealthiest and most innovative nation on earth. The Pilgrims sowed the seeds of political freedom, free enterprise, and healthy individualism in covenant with God.

Christian socialism?

How committed were these Pilgrims to their Christian faith? Unlike the British Puritans, who desired to reform the Church of England from within, the Separatists demanded a complete *separation*. They believed there were so many reforms needed in the Church that it could not possibly be accomplished to their satisfaction. They felt their only choice was to leave the state church. Due to the great persecution the Separatists suffered, many fled to Holland.

Finally a group of these Pilgrims set out for a new land for freedom of religion. Upon reaching the shores of Cape Cod, the first action taken by the Pilgrims was to draft the Mayflower Compact, forming a civil government based on covenant with God and with one another. But Christian communism didn't work even with this level of commitment to God and one another. I dare say, most of us would look shallow and carnal compared to such courage and devotion. If the Pilgrims couldn't make communism work, who could?

> ### *If the Pilgrims couldn't make communism work, who could?*

Does the Bible teach socialism?

Does the Bible encourage socialism/communism? Some people quote Acts 4:32-35 to claim Jesus taught socialism. What do these verses actually teach? First, the book of Acts Christians were supernaturally knit together into a *one accord* that was so powerful they were "of one heart and soul." Second, they had received an impartation of "great grace." The word for great in Greek is *megas*. They had received an extraordinary measure of grace, or *mega-grace*.

*Now the full number of those who believed were **of one heart and soul**, and no one said that any of the things that belonged to him was his own, but they had everything in common. And with great power the apostles were giving their testimony to resurrec-*

*tion of the Lord Jesus, and **GREAT GRACE** was upon them all [emphasis mine] (Acts 4:32-33).*

Third, they laid all they had at the feet of the *apostles* — NOT the civil government! God has given the responsibility for charitable giving to the *Church*! There is a big difference between the first century apostolic church and civil government.

*There was not a needy person among them, for as many as were owners of lands or houses sold them and brought the proceeds of what was sol⁵ and laid it at the **apostles' feet** [NOT THE CIVIL GOVERNMENT] and it was distributed to each as any had need [emphasis mine] (Acts 4:34-35).*

> ***They laid all they had at the feet of the apostles — NOT the civil government!***

Finally, this particular pattern of "all things in common" is not a pervasive pattern throughout the New Testament. It is the *exception* rather than the rule. The Bible says charity is an *individual* matter of the heart, each person deciding what to give voluntarily.

Each one must give as he has decided in his heart, not reluctantly or under compulsion, for God loves a cheerful giver (2 Corinthians 9:7).

THE CHARITY FRUIT

Are Americans more or less charitable than citizens of other countries?

No developed country even begins to approach American giving. In 1995, the most recent year for which data is available, research shows that Americans donate three-and-a-half times more to charity than the French. They give seven times more than the Germans. Fourteen times more than the Italians. Americans are 15 percent more likely to volunteer time to help others than the Dutch, 21 percent more likely than the Swiss, and 32 percent more likely than the Germans.

Who really cares?

In his book, *Who Really Cares: The Surprising Truth About Compassionate Conservatism*, Arthur C. Brooks presents research showing religious conservatives (those who attend church regularly) are much more charitable, compassionate, and willing to volunteer than secular liberals.[6]

Who really cares? Individuals who lean toward socialism give almost none of their *own* money to charity. They just like to give away other people's money. Those who believe *government* should redistribute income are among the *least likely* to donate, volunteer, or help others in any way. Individuals who are religious American *capitalists* turn out to be the biggest givers of all. In an analysis of fifteen sets of data, the conclusion was always the same.

> ### *Individuals who lean toward socialism give almost none of their own money to charity.*

Religious American capitalists are much more likely to be generous to those in need than those who believe in socialism. They are twenty-three times more likely to volunteer their time to assist others than socialists. Religious Americans who believe in capitalism give 75 percent more to charity than Americans who believe in socialism.

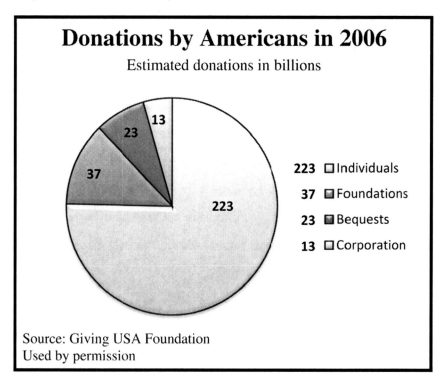

Donations by Americans in 2006
Estimated donations in billions

223 □ Individuals
37 ■ Foundations
23 ■ Bequests
13 □ Corporation

Source: Giving USA Foundation
Used by permission

THE LIFE OR DEATH FRUIT

Jesus came to set the captives free and bring abundant *life* to mankind. The enemy steals, *kills*, and destroys. The true nature of any philosophy can be determined by examining historical evidence to see what happens when it is implemented. Does it produce life. . .or death?

> *I am the door. If anyone enters by Me, he will be saved, and will go in and out and find pasture. **The thief does not come except to steal, and to KILL, and to destroy. I have come that they may have LIFE**, and that they may have it more abundantly [emphasis mine] (John 10:9-11).*

Although socialism and communism had been attempted by small, isolated groups previously, there had never before been a communist government with actual power over the citizens until Vladimir Lenin (1870–1924). What Marx and Engels had proposed in *The Communist Manifesto* was embraced with murderous zeal by Lenin. For the first time, communist revolutionaries became determined to implement communism by force.

POWER KILLS; absolute power kills absolutely [emphasis mine].[7]

–R. J. Rummel

Lenin was a Russian revolutionary, economic theorist, lawyer, and political philosopher who created the Soviet Communist Party and led the Bolshevik Revolution of 1917 in Russia. "Lenin condemned the peasants to be the mere building blocks of the Communist edifice that he had fixed in his mind. It was the peasants who bore the brunt of the civil war. . . This was the path to Lenin's cooperative plan and socialist industrialization. It was for this, according to him, that people were shot in the thousands."[8, 9]

> *"Lenin condemned the peasants to be the mere building blocks of the Communist edifice that he had fixed in his mind."*

Mass executions, artificially created famines, slave labor and death camps (gulags), and forced migrations of whole racial and ethnic groups were responsible for possibly 1,000,000 deaths. Lenin's violent and crude language coupled with a total lack of conscience "escalated into the physical elimination of all those who chose not to fall into line, and. . . once absorbed as normal behaviour by the Party, this became an integral and essential feature of the regime in its post-Lenin years."[10] If Lenin had not died at the relatively young age of fifty-three, the numbers of those murdered would certainly have been much higher.

Joseph Stalin (1878-1953) succeeded Lenin in power as the Premier of the Soviet Union. Stalin continued and intensified the violent brutality, ultimately bringing the total killed to an estimated

61,911,000. This is more than the total number deliberately killed by governments for all recorded history prior to the 20th century. Stalin continued the practice of deliberately causing *man-made famines*. This later became a standard tool of communist terror. Stalin was responsible for murdering 333,000 men, women, and children by forced starvation alone. The main goal of this artificial famine/genocide was to break the spirit of the farmers and peasants to force them into collectivization.

The first century of the modern age was unprecedented in cruelty and horror caused by communists. Communism is clearly based in love for power and love of an ideology—not love for people. Genuine love does not murder.

Watch what God does, and then you do it, like children who learn proper behavior from their parents. Mostly what God does is love you. Keep company with Him and learn a life of love. Observe how Christ loved us. His love was not cautious but extravagant. He didn't love in order to get something from us but to give everything of himself to us. Love like that (Ephesians 5:1-2 MSG).

Excerpt from
"The Red Plague"
by R. J. Rummel

How can we understand all this killing by communists? It is the marriage of an absolutist ideology with the absolute power. Communists believed that they knew the truth, absolutely. They believed that they knew through Marxism what would bring about the greatest human welfare and happiness. And they believed that power, the dictatorship of the proletariat, must be used to tear down the old feudal or capitalist order and rebuild society and culture to realize this utopia. Nothing must stand in the way of its achievement. . . .

Government--the Communist Party--was thus above any law. All institutions, cultural norms, traditions, and sentiments were expendable. And the people were as though lumber and bricks, to be used in building the new world.

[T]o many communists, the cause of a communist utopia was such as to justify all the deaths. The irony of this is that communism in practice, even after decades of total control, did not improve the lot of the average person, but usually made their living conditions worse than before the revolution. . . . Communism has been the greatest social engineering experiment we have ever seen. It failed utterly and in doing so it killed over 100,000,000 men, women, and children, not to mention the near 30,000,000 of its subjects that died in its often aggressive wars and the rebellions it provoked. . . .

But there is a larger lesson to be learned from this horrendous sacrifice to one ideology. That is that **no one can be trusted with power. . . . The more power the center has to impose the beliefs of an ideological or religious elite or impose the whims of a dictator, the more likely human lives are to be sacrificed.** This is but one reason, but perhaps the most important one, for fostering. . . democracy [emphasis mine].[11]

Democide

R. J. Rummel, professor emeritus of political science at the University of Hawaii, coined the word *democide,* meaning "the deliberate murder of its own citizens by a government." His entire career has been dedicated to researching violence and war, with the goal of finding a solution for war, genocide and democide. According to Rummel's research, six times as many people died of deliberate democide during the 20th century than in all the wars that took place during that period of time.

In total, during the first eighty-eight years of [the 20th century], almost 170 million men, women, and children have been shot, beaten, tortured, knifed, burned, starved, frozen, crushed, or worked to death; buried alive, drowned, hung, bombed, or killed in any other of the myriad ways governments have inflicted death on unarmed, helpless citizens and foreigners. The dead could conceivably be nearly 360 million people. It is as though our species has been devastated by a modern Black Plague. And indeed it has, but a plague of Power, not germs.[12]

> *"It is as though our species has been devastated by a modern Black Plague. And indeed it has, but a plague of Power, not germs."*

Estimated total killed by all tyrannical governments, 1900-1999 = 262,000,000

The battle of our time is truly a *war* for economic control. Who would have dreamed that economic ideology could unleash the most dreadful killing machine in the history of the world? Unfortunately, innocent citizens are considered expendable "building materials" in this war.

Communist governments were responsible for the democide of **169,198,000** men, women, and children between 1900-1999. The actual number is probably much higher. In *The Black Book of Communism*, Stéphane Courtois writes, "[C]ommunist regimes, in order to consolidate their grip on power, turned mass crime into a full-blown system of government."[13] Communists are convinced mass extermination is a "necessary tool" for implementing their ideology.

Old and young, healthy and sick, men and women, even infants and the infirm, were killed in cold blood. They were not combatants in civil war or rebellions; they were not criminals. Indeed, nearly all were guilty of. . . nothing.[14]

Total killed by Communists 1900-1999 = 169,198,000

The **world total** of individuals deliberately murdered by governments between 1900-1999 totals approximately **262,000,000**.

The bodies of these victims would encircle the earth ten times if they were laid head to toe.

World total killed by governments 1900-1999 = 262,000,000

Hitler was an amateur

Everyone knows about the Holocaust and Adolf Hitler, but compared to the communist megamurderers, Hitler was just an amateur! Although the communists have successfully distanced themselves from the Third Reich, fascism is very closely aligned with the ideology of communism/socialism. "NAZI" is an acronym for the first two words of the National *Socialist* German Workers' Party. Examine the numbers killed in Soviet Russia and China to those murdered by Hitler. The most commonly quoted estimate is 6,000,000 Jews and 14,000,000 non-Jews. Mao and Stalin were far worse.

Hitler Jews	6,000,000
non-Jews	14,000,000
Mao Zedong (China)	76,000,000
Soviet Russia	61,911,000

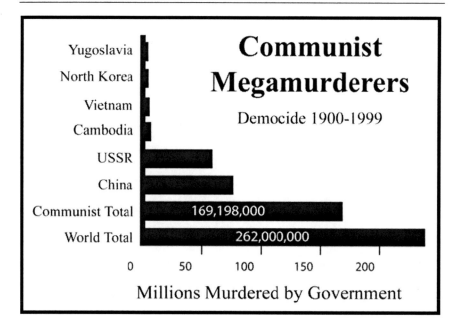

Source: R. J. Rummel [15]

The Holodomor

During 1932-33, Stalin ordered a man-made famine to crush the spirit of Ukraine. The Ukrainian peasants were individualists who proudly resisted subjugation. For the communists, collectivizing agriculture as a tool of domination. It is imposed forcefully upon the oppressed peoples to master them. Collectivization is a more a political ideology than economic policy, a means of stifling private initiative and gaining total control.

The communists, beginning with Lenin and Stalin, were the first to use the weapon of starvation as a tool to dominate and eliminate people. One horrifying example is the Holodomor [literally translated from Ukrainian as "death by starvation"] in the Ukraine during 1932-33.

The breadbasket of the old tsarist empire, Ukraine, was now to feed the proletariat of Moscow and Petrograd. Requisitioning quotas were higher there than anywhere else in the Soviet empire. To meet them would have been to condemn thousands of villages. . .to certain starvation. . . . This policy, which aimed to transform the great sugar- and grain-producing areas into huge collective farms with the peasants as nothing more than agricultural laborers.[16]

> **The Bolsheviks sealed the borders of the nation to make it impossible for peasants to escape or food supplies to come in.**

The grain procurement quota (grain taken to supply cities and troops) was raised to an astronomical level, knowing it would cause a grain shortage, which would, in turn, leave the peasants without enough food to survive.[17] When the starvation began, the Bolsheviks sealed the borders of the nation to make it impossible for peasants to escape or food supplies to come in.

Soviet-controlled granaries were said to be bursting at the seams from huge stocks of 'reserve' grain, which had not yet been shipped out of the Ukraine. In some locations, grain and potatoes were piled in the open, protected by barbed wire and armed GPU [Cheka] guards who shot down anyone attempting to take the food. Farm animals, considered necessary for production, were allowed to be fed, while the people living among them had absolutely nothing to eat.

By the spring of 1933, the height of the famine, an estimated 25,000 persons died every day in the Ukraine. Entire villages were perishing. In Europe, America and Canada, persons of Ukrainian descent and others responded to news reports of the famine by sending in food supplies. But Soviet authorities halted all food shipments at the border.[18]

Eyewitness accounts

A survivor of the Holodomor, Miron Dolot, describes the horrors of the famine he faced as a young Ukrainian boy in his book, *Execution by Hunger*:

Thus this monstrous machine of collectivization was set in motion. It ground, it pulled, it pushed, and it kicked. It was run by human beings, and it worked on human beings. It was merciless and insatiable. Once it started, it could not be stopped, and it consumed more and more victims.[19]

The heroic Soviet Communist defector, Victor Kravchenko, wrote of his experiences of life in the Soviet Union and as a whistle-blower Soviet official. His 1946 book, *I Chose Freedom*, describes the prison camps and collectivization. He writes:

Although not a word about the tragedy appeared in the newspapers, the famine that raged. . . was a matter of common knowledge. What I saw that morning. . . was inexpressibly horrible. On a battlefield men die quickly, they fight back. Here I saw people dying in solitude by slow degrees, dying hideously, without the excuse of sacrifice for a cause. They had been trapped and left to starve, each in his own home, by a political decision made in a far off capital around conference and banquet tables.

> *"They had been trapped and left to starve, each in his own home, by a political decision made in a far off capital around conference and banquet tables."*

There was not even the consolation of inevitability to relieve the horror. The most terrifying sights were the little children, with skeleton limbs, dangling from balloon-like abdomens. Starvation had wiped every trace of youth from their faces, turning them into tortured gargoyles; only in their eyes, still lingered the reminder of childhood. Everywhere we found men and women lying prone, weak from hunger, their faces and bellies bloated, their eyes utterly expressionless. Yet at the very time these Belsen-like scenes were being enacted in Ukraine, food was being sent not to the starving but out of the country. . . .

We knocked at a door and received no reply. . . . Fearfully I pushed the door open. . . into the one room hut. . . . The nightmarishness of the scene was not the corpse on the bed, but in the condition of the living witnesses. The old woman's legs were blown up to an incredible size, the man and children were clearly in the last stages of starvation. . . . In an adjoining house. . . a gaunt woman was busy at the stove.

"What are you cooking, Natalka?" Chadai asked her. "You know what I'm cooking," she answered, and in her voice there was a murderous fury. "Why did she get so angry?" I asked. "Because— well, I'm ashamed to tell you, Victor Andreyevich. . . . She's cooking horse manure and weeds."[20]

Kravchenko continues:

In bed that night, I thought of the new privileged class in the village—the Party and Soviet functionaries who were receiving milk and butter and supplies from the cooperative shop while everyone else around them starved. Slavishly they obeyed orders from the center, indifferent to the suffering of the common people. The corruption of character by privilege was fearsome to behold; these men who only a few years ago were themselves poor peasants had already lost the last trace of identification with their neighbors. . . . Some of the peasants might not be able to write, but all of them understood the injustice only too well. "Socialism," they sneered. "Robbery is a better name for it."[21]

In 2008, Kravchenko's son, Andrew, released a documentary film, *The Defector*, which is an extraordinary chronicle of his father's passion, sacrifices, and ultimate victory in his struggle to expose the crimes of the ruthless Josef Stalin.

Media complicity

The tragedy in Ukrainian countryside was masterfully disguised by the Soviet propagandists and journalists. European and American media were complicit in the deception. Left-leaning intellectuals, such as George Bernard Shaw, approved of any means to further the cause of the communists. Communists fully understood the media must be controlled. The British press provided selective coverage, but the Ukrainian famine was almost invisible in foreign newspapers. Walter Duranty (1884-1957), Stalinist sympathizer and correspondent for the New York Times, was a master of the Ukraine "cover up." He was later awarded a Pulitzer Prize for writing lies.

Duranty skirted the truth and had some of the densest and circu-
itous reporting that could be found. To reporters in Moscow he
was known as Walter Obscuranty.[22]

Most journalists in Russia were either too afraid to speak out or
in silent agreement with events taking place. Another hurdle, should
anyone dare to write the truth, was getting stories past the censors.

> ## *The European and American media were complicit in the deception.*

The heroism of Malcom Muggeridge

Malcolm Muggeridge (1903-1990), British freelance journalist
without fixed position or income, was initially attracted by the ideals
of communism, but became increasingly disillusioned. When he
heard conflicting reports about Ukrainian food shortages, he became
determined to learn the truth about what was happening and, despite
a travel ban, bought a train ticket to the Ukraine. Amazingly, Muggeridge was able to get into the country and investigate without
official observation. No one knew his plans and no Soviet officials
tried to stop him. If he had been caught, he would have been killed.
Muggeridge saw the horrors of villages abandoned, the absence of
livestock, emaciated, frightened people and terrified rope-bound
peasants who were herded into cattle cars at gun-point.[23]

After witnessing the horrors of the famine firsthand, he disguised his dispatches in diplomatic pouches. Walter Duranty, and many other journalists who were also communist sympathizers, denounced his reports, calling them fabrications. Years later, Muggeridge was vindicated and his reports proved true.

Malcolm Muggeridge went to Russia believing in the promise of communism, but left believing in the existence of evil.[24]

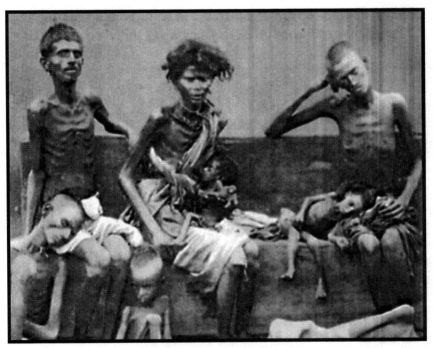

Starving Ukranian Family [25]

Hear this, you elders; listen, all who
live in the land. Has anything like this
ever happened in your days or in the
days of your forefathers? Tell it to your

children, and let your children tell it to their children, and their children to the next generation (Joel 1:2-3).

"Bad harvest"

Former Ukrainian President Victor Yuschenko laments:

[The Holodomor] was a state-organized program of mass starvation that in 1932-33 killed an estimated seven to ten million Ukrainians, including up to a third of the nation's children. With grotesque understatement the Soviet authorities dismissed this event as a "bad harvest."[25]

A *bad harvest* indeed!

A bad harvest indeed!

Could it happen again?

Larry Grathwohl, an undercover FBI agent who infiltrated the Weather Underground during the 1970s, said that the "most bone-chilling" thing he heard was a comment by Bill Ayers that an estimated 25 million Americans would probably need to be exterminated to overthrow the American government.[27] 25,000,000 dead bodies, if placed head to toe in straight lines, would go all the way across America nearly eight times from the Atlantic to the Pacific Oceans.

Fear is the foundation of most governments. –John Adams, Thoughts on Government, 1776

The "Freedom Formula" for world peace

Why do people smile when beauty pageant contestants answer the question, "What is the most important thing society needs?" by saying "world peace"? Because everyone knows she does not have a clue what she is talking about, and there is no way she could actually contribute to *world peace*. So, what *can* bring the longed-for world peace to mankind?

The Founding Fathers of America discovered the true answer for peace. Freedom is a right given by God. It leads to economic prosperity, and decreases hunger and famine. Free people do not go to war with other free nations. Free governments do not kill innocent citizens.

The solution is freedom!

NOTE: Every genocide and democide of the 20th century was preceded by gun control and disarmament of civilians.

[The Constitution preserves] the advantage of being armed which Americans possess over the people of almost every other

nation. . .(where) the governments are afraid to trust the people with arms. –James Madison, The Federalist Papers, No. 46.

I ask, Sir, what is the militia? It is the whole people. To disarm the people is the best and most effectual way to enslave them. *–George Mason, Co-author of the Second Amendment during Virginia's Convention to Ratify the Constitution, 1788*

The U.S. Bill of Rights Article II

A well regulated militia, being necessary to the security of a free state, the right of the people to keep and bear arms, shall not be infringed.

Chapter Seven
Discussion Questions

1. What happens when the standard of living improves for individuals?
2. What is the benefit of a large middle class?
3. The necessary ingredients for creativity are an atmosphere that:

   •

   •

   •

4. How does socialism punish creativity?

5. How does free enterprise reward creativity?

6. Is it true that we are using up the planet's natural resources?

7. What is a natural resource without man's creativity?

8. What is the most valuable resource?

9. Explain socialism's "pie" argument? Explain capitalism's "pie" response.

10. Compare and contrast how the early American settlers fared under socialism/communism as opposed to free enterprise in the Jamestown and Plymouth colonies.

11. How charitable are individuals with their own money who lean toward socialism/communism with their own money?

12. Who are the most generous Americans? Why do you think this is true?

13. Why is power in the hands of government so dangerous?

14. What is the estimated total killed by Communist governments between 1900-1999?

15. Why do you think the media helped hide the Holodomor from the world?

Chapter 8

FREEDOM AND FREE ENTERPRISE

*A*merica became God's model of freedom for the whole world. The twin blessings of liberty and free enterprise offer hope to oppressed people worldwide. The poem inscribed on the base of the Statue of Liberty refers not to immigration but to Lady Liberty's torch lighting the way to the "golden door" of freedom and opportunity. The door is not just America herself, but a *freedom formula* for other nations to copy. The following inscription was mounted on the lower level of the pedestal of the Statue of Liberty in 1903:

> *. . . Give me your tired, your poor, your huddled masses yearning to breathe free, the wretched refuse of your teeming shore. Send these, the homeless, tempest-tossed to me, I lift my lamp beside the golden door!*
>
> –"The New Colossus" by Emma Lazarus

Freedom had been hunted round the globe; reason was consid-ered as rebellion; and the slavery of fear had made men afraid to think. But such is the irresistible nature of truth, that all it asks, and all it wants, is the liberty of appearing.

–Thomas Paine, Rights of Man, 1791

The Declaration of Independence

The Declaration of Independence [is the] declaratory charter of our rights, and the rights of man.

–Thomas Jefferson, letter to S. A. Wells, May 12, 1821.

Because of the Founding Fathers of America, you have an oppor-tunity that few people have ever had in human history — the opportu-nity to be free. Our Founders did not believe man should live under tyranny. God Himself created all men equal with God-given rights. It is God's plan for men to be free. Jesus Himself said that He came to "set the captives free."

The purpose of government is to protect the rights of citizens to life, liberty, and property. The Declaration of Independence empha-sizes the authority of a government is granted by the *consent of the governed*. Therefore, the Preamble of the U.S. Constitution begins with the bold words, "**We the People**."

THE DECLARATION OF INDEPENDENCE

When in the Course of human events it becomes necessary for one people to dissolve the political bands which have connected them with another and to assume among the powers of the earth, the separate and equal station to which the Laws of Nature and of Nature's God entitle them, a decent respect to the opinions of mankind requires that they should declare the causes which impel them to the separation.

We hold these truths to be self-evident, that all men are created equal, that they are endowed by their Creator with certain inalienable Rights, that among these are Life, Liberty and the pursuit of Happiness. ***That to secure these rights, Governments are instituted among Men, deriving their just powers from the consent of the governed [emphasis mine]. . .***

1. **Laws of Nature**

   The universal and eternal laws of God (Divine Law) rule over men and nations.

2. **Nature's God**

   There is one good and omnipotent God (Nature's God) who rules universally and eternally, judging the affairs of men. Because God is good and His law Absolute, it is man's duty to love God and people.

3. **Self -evident truths**

   God has revealed His truths to man and their authenticity is indisputable. These truths are rational, obvious, and morally good.

4. **Equality**

   Men are created equal in God's sight, equal in their rights, and equal in the eyes of justice. They should have equal opportunity, but are not guaranteed equal outcomes.

5. **Inalienable rights**

   God Himself is the one who gave rights to man. No one can take them away or violate them without coming under the judgment of God. Other rights may be created by statute as "vested" rights, but vested rights are not inalienable. They can be altered or eliminated.

6. **Life, liberty, and the pursuit of happiness**
   God gave rights to life, liberty, and property.
7. **Purpose of government**
   The purpose of government is to protect and preserve the God-given rights of citizens.
8. **Consent of the governed**
   No government has a right to exist except by the consent of the people.

> ### *The purpose of government is to protect the rights of citizens to life, liberty, and property.*

A free people [claim] their rights as derived from the laws of nature [laws of God], and not as the gift of their chief magistrate.

–Thomas Jefferson, Rights of British America, 1774

And can the liberties of a nation be thought secure when we have removed their only firm basis, a conviction in the minds of the people that these liberties are the gift of God? That they are not to be violated but with his wrath? Indeed I tremble for my country when I reflect that God is just: that his justice cannot sleep for ever.

–Thomas Jefferson, Notes on the State of Virginia,

Query 18, 1781

The most sacred of the duties of a government [is] to do equal and impartial justice to all citizens.

–Thomas Jefferson, Note in Destutt de Tracy, 1816

Birth of a Free Nation

When the Declaration of Independence was signed in 1776, an extraordinary event had occurred in the annals of world history. It was the birth of a free nation. The grand American experiment began—to show the world man *can* govern himself!

We recognize no Sovereign but God, and no King but Jesus!

–John Adams and John Hancock, April 18, 1775

Accomplishment of American Independence

- **George Washington:** *The preservation of the sacred fire of liberty, and the destiny of the Republican model of government are justly considered as deeply, perhaps as finally staked, on the experiment entrusted to the hands of the American people.*

  –First Inaugural Address, April 30, 1789

- **James Madison:** *Happily for America, happily we trust for the whole human race, they pursued a new and more noble course. They accomplished a revolution that has no parallel in* *the annals of human society. . . .In Europe, charters of liberty have been granted by power. America has set the example. . . of charters of power granted by liberty.*

–Federalist No. 14, November 20, 1787

- **James Madison:** *In Europe, charters of liberty have been granted by power. America has set the example. . .of charters of power granted by liberty. This revolution in the practice of the world, may, with an honest praise, be pronounced the most triumphant epoch of its history, and the most consoling presage of its happiness.*

  –National Gazette Essay, January 18, 1792

- **John Quincy Adams:** *The highest glory of the American Revolution was this: it connected in one indissoluble bond the principles of civil government with the principles of Christianity.*

  –From a speech, July 4, 1821

The Liberty Bell

Bells rang out throughout America to mark the reading of the Declaration of Independence on July 8, 1776. Tradition has it that the day the Declaration of Independence was signed, the Liberty Bell in Philadelphia, Pennsylvania was rung. The Hebrew year of

Jubilee occurred every fifty years and provided restoration of personal liberty and restitution of property. Part of the scripture verse Leviticus 25:10, announcing the year of Jubilee, inscribed on the bell:

Proclaim LIBERTY throughout all the land unto all the inhabitants thereof [emphasis mine].

Revolution and crisis

America had won the Revolutionary War, but now the fledgling nation was in crisis! The British army waited on the borders, planning to rush back in and seize power when the whole thing fell apart at the seams. Most of the soldiers in the Continental Army had never been paid, the states seemed incapable of agreeing on anything, and the economy was in shambles.

Not only was there unrest in the military, with many soldiers and officers wanting to name George Washington king or military dictator, but the country was in economic chaos. Because of rampant unemployment, people were not able to pay for the necessities of life, so scores of citizens were losing their land, homes, livestock, and even the basic household necessities. Mobs began forming, much like those that had rebelled against the former oppressive British rulers.

> ## *America had won the Revolutionary War, but now the fledgling nation was in crisis!*

The Constitution of the United States of America

No nation had ever before forged a democratic republic. The Founders had no model to copy. They knew that The Articles of Confederation had been wholly inadequate during the war. Finally, due to the faithfulness and perseverance of George Washington, the states agreed to call a Constitutional Convention. The Framers of the Constitution later called it a miracle that the Convention had even taken place, and called the Constitution itself a miracle.

The happy union of these States is a wonder; their Constitution a miracle; their example the hope of Liberty throughout the world.
–James Madison, Outline, September 1829

It appears to me, then, little short of a miracle, that the Delegates from so many different States. . . should unite in forming a system of national Government, so little liable to well founded objections.
–George Washington, letter to Marquis de Lafayette, February 7, 1788

Now what?

With the foundation of civil government laid, the Founders found it necessary to turn their attention to economics. America was exhausted, depleted, and deeply in debt. The American colonies had been British dependents for over 150 years. They had absolutely no experience in economic development. Financial resources were limited, they had almost no manufacturing capability, and no banks. The Founding Fathers, especially Benjamin Franklin, James Madison, and Alexander Hamilton turned to Adam Smith for a plan.

The Wealth of Nations

Adam Smith (1723-1790), taught and wrote about ethics and the rights and duties of individuals. In 1773, he moved to London and continued his writing. In 1776, at the age of 53, Smith published *An Inquiry into the Nature and Causes of the Wealth of Nations*, a modern blueprint for economic success! At the exact time that America became a sovereign nation, a strategy for the nation's economy was provided.

Blueprint for economic success

Adam Smith had spent years studying the nature and cause of a nation's prosperity. He had observed that government intervention has a detrimental effect on the creation of wealth. However, freedom unleashed individual effort and creativity, because free individuals protected by just laws create prosperous and inventive societies.

My God! How little do my countrymen know what precious blessings they are in possession of, and which no other people on earth enjoy!

–Thomas Jefferson, letter to James Monroe, June 17, 1785

Creating national wealth

Wealth is automatically created in a nation when certain conditions are met. These conditions are a low level of interference from the government, protection of private property, and low taxes.

The necessary conditions for wealth creation are:

- Low level of government regulation
- Protection of private property
- Low taxes

Free individuals protected by just laws create prosperous and inventive societies.

Four principles of social interaction

Smith observed four principles of social interaction that led to prosperity when accompanied by freedom: healthy self-interest, division of labor, competition, and benefit of society.

1. Healthy self-interest

When people are free to make a living under a system of just laws, they strive to succeed, provide for their families, and cooperate with one another. This mutual cooperation is beneficial to everyone involved.

2. Division of labor

Quality and efficiency are increased when each worker becomes an expert in one area of production, based on personal interest and aptitude.

3. Competition

Competition is an "invisible hand" guiding a free market by competition for resources. No outside regulation of any type is needed, because competition automatically improves products and lowers prices.

4. Society as a whole benefits

Free individuals and free markets create wealth for both individuals and the nation, and raise the standard of living of poor citizens at the same time.

BACK TO YOUR NEIGHBORHOOD

Do you remember the predicament of your neighborhood in chapter one? Conditions have deteriorated ever since the HOA took control. The economy of the neighborhood has been devastated. Most people no longer work because it just isn't worth it. Wages are low, taxes are high, jobs are scarce. Many people are suffering from depression. Some activists gather secretly in basements to vent their anger.

Finally, it is time for those in power to face election day. No one dared voted the scoundrels out of office for years because they were afraid to lose all their benefits. But now, the HOA has finally run out of everyone else's money and have had to cut back on entitlements. The HOA reneged on their promises. The neighborhood is broke.

People take a good look around at the devastation that used to be their beautiful neighborhood. The formerly manicured lawns are completely overgrown with weeds. The roads are full of potholes. The homes are in desperate need of repair, cars and bicycles are broken down, and most of the shops are boarded up.

> **"Considering the natural lust for power so inherent in man, I fear the thirst of power will prevail to oppress the people."**

A new beginning

You and all your neighbors realize that you have been conned! Everyone in the neighborhood rises up, heads to the ballot box, and throws the bums out. You vote in a new government committed to re-establishing a constitution and by-laws with checks and balances for the leaders. Next, with a new government in place, the neighborhood begins to implement a plan to create neighborhood wealth!

Freedom: The new government follows the Founders' freedom formula and requires self-reliance and personal responsibility on the part of the citizens.

New Rules:
- Private property.
- Everyone must work.
- If you don't work, you don't eat.

Free Enterprise: The neighborhood adopts the "Adam Smith" economic plan.
- Protection of private property

- Low taxes
- Low level of government regulations

The following social interaction takes place:

1. Healthy self-interest

Joe starts an auto repair shop in his garage. Joe repairs Mitch and Katie's car. They pay Joe with their home-grown vegetables. Mitch and Katie begin driving to another neighborhood and sell some vegetables. They start a shuttle service for a few people who want to commute to work in other neighborhoods. They earn enough money to pay Joe for repairing their cars.

More and more people begin to earn money, then use that money to start businesses in the empty buildings, and hire employees. Joe is able to hire four assistants and rent a building. Joe is also able to do a minor repair on Karla's washing machine, who then starts a small laundry service in her home. Local home repair and lawn service businesses are launched. More and more people can afford to purchase items locally.

2. Division of labor

Kris and Martha start a bakery. At first they do most of the work, including cleaning. They hire an expert pastry chef and a cake decorator and the word gets out. Their business grows, so they hire someone to deliver wedding cakes and another person to do clean up. That frees up their time, so they spend less time in the kitchen and begin to open franchises in nearby locales.

3. Competition

Julia starts a bakery, too. She adds a party planning service on the side, and offers complete party packages in addition to cakes and pastries. Kris and Martha lose some business, so they cut prices on breads and bagels. Julia cuts some prices, too. Customers like lower prices.

Kris and Martha add some tables and open a small sandwich section for lunch. They streamline their production, which cuts their operating costs, so they can lower prices even more. The whole neighborhood enjoys the lower prices and increased options.

4. Society as a whole benefits

As more and more businesses open up and hire more workers, the entire neighborhood begins to prosper. New people start moving to the neighborhood and buying homes. New roads are built, old roads are paved, and several rich couples build large new homes. Property value goes up for everyone! The whole neighborhood is glad to welcome them.

Mr. and Mrs. Ritzy enjoy living in the nice neighborhood and spend a lot of money at the local shops. They also want to be a blessing to their community. The Ritzys open a shelter for abused and disadvantaged women, in addition to becoming major financial contributors for the local hospital. But they don't just give charitable donations. The Ritzys also hire a sizeable staff to work at the shelter and teach job skills to help people get back on their feet.

It is a Jubilee for your neighborhood. You and your neighbors were economic slaves and now you are free!

Captivity or freedom

Socialism began in the Garden of Eden from the tree of the knowledge of good and evil when man began to rely on human reason apart from God. Socialism/communism is a total social, economic, political, and spiritual system, which calls good evil and evil good. It is not just a difference of opinion, economic theory, politics, or ideologies. The end result is destruction, not paradise.

The great American experiment in civil government and economics, both based in freedom, quickly made America the strongest, wealthiest, and freest nation in the world. The Framers of the Constitution attempted to limit the power of the federal government through checks and balances.

George Mason, the Father of the Bill of Rights, said, "Considering the natural lust for power so inherent in man, I fear the thirst of power will prevail to oppress the people." Mason was right. Every handout from the government is accompanied by more regulations, less individual liberty, and greater oppression. In his 1989 farewell address, Ronald Reagan stated, "Man is not free unless government is limited. . . . As government expands, liberty contracts."[1]

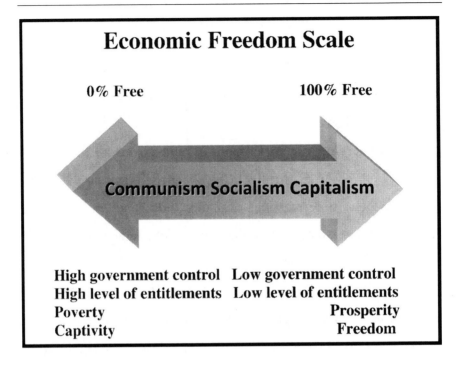

Who is a true American?

We must never sacrifice freedom for seductive promises. Now is the time to stand up and be a true American in every sense of the word. A true American is a person who has the same heart and values as the Founding Fathers of America and cherishes freedom and free enterprise for the benefit of all mankind.

"Man is not free unless government is limited. . . . As government expands, liberty contracts."

What can you do?

Start by knowing the truth yourself. Next, get the word out. Teach the lessons of this book to your children and grandchildren. Share what you have learned with family, friends and neighbors. Get involved with other lovers of freedom. And buy a copy of this book to give to someone else!

Happily for America, happily, we trust, for the whole human race, they pursued a new and more noble course. They accomplished a revolution which has no parallel in the annals of human society. They reared the fabrics of governments which have no model on the face of the globe. They formed the design of a great Confederacy, which it is incumbent on their successors to improve and perpetuate. –James Madison, Federalist No. 14, November 30, 1787

Our country is in danger, but not to be despaired of. Our enemies are numerous and powerful; but we have many friends, determining to be free, and heaven and earth will aid the resolution. On you depends the fortunes of America. You are to decide the important question, on which rest the happiness and liberty of millions yet unborn. Act worthy of yourselves. –Joseph Warren, Boston Massacre Oration, March 6, 1775

Chapter Eight
Action Steps

- Start by knowing the truth yourself.

- Stay informed about what is going on in our nation.

- Teach the lessons of this book to your children and grandchildren.

- Share what you have learned with family, friends and neighbors.

- Invite others to study the book in small groups (and listen to the CDs or watch the videos together.) ***Was Jesus a Capitalist* CD and DVD sets are available online at www.forgive123. com**.

- Join other lovers of freedom and become active online, or in your community.

- Buy an extra copy of this book to give away!

NOTES

1. GOOD NEWS OF FREEDOM

1   Thatcher, M. (1976). From an interview with journalist Llew Gardner for Thames television's *This Week* program on November 5, 1976. Retrieved July 17, 2011 from http://www.margaretthatcher.org /speeches/displaydocument.asp?docid=102953

2   Valdnieks, K. (Producer) & Snore, E. (Director), Daugavvanags, E. (Cinematography) (2010). The Soviet Story [DVD]. Latvia: SIA Labvakar.

3   LeBon, G. (1925). *The Crowd*. New York, NY: The Macmillan Co. pp. 4-6.

4   Bernays, E. (2005). *Propaganda*. Brooklyn, NY: IG Publishing. Originally published 1928. pp. 37-39.

2. GOOD NEWS OF FREEDOM

1   Redleaf, A. and Vigilante, R. (2010). *Panic: The Betrayal of Capitalism by Wall Street and Washington*. Minneapolis, MN: Richard Vigilante Books. p. 8.

4. TEST BY HISTORY

1   Smith, A. (1776). *The Wealth of Nations, Volumes I-III*. Reprinted in 1986. New York, NY: Penguin Books. p. 14.

2   Sowell, T. (2009). *Intellectuals and Society*. New York, NY: Basic Books. pp. 1-9.

3   Butler, A. (1980). Josiah Warren and the Sovereignty of the Individual. *The Journal of Libertarian Studies*, Vol. IV, No. 4.

4   Bernstein, E. (9161). *Evolutionary Socialism: A Criticism and Affirmation*. New York, NY: Random House.

5. TEST BY THE SPIRIT

1   Durant, W. and Durant, A. (1967). *The Story of Civilization*. Vol. X, Rousseau and Revolution. New York, NY: Simon and Schuster. pp. 902-903.

6. TEST BY THE WORD OF GOD

1   Wesley, J. (1991). *John Wesley's Sermons: An Anthology*. The Use of Money (1760). Nashville, TN: Abingdon Press. pp. 347-358.

2   Webster, N. (1828). *An American Dictionary of the English Language*. New York, NY: S. Converse. s.v. "property."

3   Dickinson, J. (1801). *The Political Writings of John Dickinson*. Wilmington, DE: Bonsal and Niles. Vol. I, p. p. 275.

4   Vander Laan, R. (2009). *Life and Ministry of the Messiah Discovery Guide*. Grand Rapids, MI: Zondervan. p. 122.

5   Ibid., pp. 34-35.

6   Ibid., p. 189.

7   Gower, R. (1987). *The New Manners and Customs of Bible Times*. Chicago, IL: The Moody Bible Institute of Chicago. pp. 38-39.

8   Ibid, 5, p. 122.

9   Lambert, L. (1981). *Israel: The Unique Land, The Unique People*. Carol Stream, IL: Tyndale House Living Books. p. 48.

10 Ibid., 5, pp. 189-190.

11 Ibid., 5, p. 122.

7. TEST BY THE FRUIT

1   Miller, T. & Holmes, K. (2010). Economic freedom and standard of living. 2010 Index of Economic Freedom (Washington, D.C.: The Heritage Foundation and Dow Jones & Company, Inc. 2010) at heritage.org/index: World Bank, World Development Indicators (November 10, 2009). Retrieved September 4, 2011 from http://publications.worldbank.org/WDI

2   Simon, J. (1996). *The Ultimate Resource 2*. Princeton, NJ: Princeton University Press. pp. 23-40, 162-197.

3   The Story of Stuff, Referenced and Annotated Script. Retrieved September 2, 2010 from http://www.storyof stuff. com/pdfs/ annie_leonard_footnoted_script.pdf.

4   Boudreaux, D. (2001). "Human Creativity: Resources Don't Exist Until Humans Make Them Useful." The Freeman-Ideas on Liberty, March 2001, Volume: 51. Issue: 3.

5   Stossel, J. (April 4,2011). "Government creates poverty." Washington Examiner. Monday, October 3, 2011. Retrieved October 3, 2011 from http://washingtonexaminer.com/opinion/ columnists/2011/04/   american-indians-demonstrate-how-government-help-creates-   poverty?sms_ss=twitter&at_ xt=4dbafffcc9b29ca4,0.

6   Brooks, A. (2007). *Who Really Cares: The Surprising Truth about Compassionate Conservatism*. New York, NY: Basic

Books, Perseus Books Group. Originally published 2006 by Basic Books.

7   Rummel, R. J. (2004). *Death by Government*. Brunswick, NJ: Transaction Publishers. Originally published 1994. p. 1.

8   Volkogonov, D. (1994). *Lenin: A New Biography*. New York, NY: The Free Press. Translation 1994 by Harold Shukman. p. 478.

9   Lenin, V. (2004). *Collected Works of V. I. Lenin Completely Revised Edited and Annotated Part 20*. Whitefish, MT: Kessinger Publishing. Translated by Joshua Kunitz and Moissaye J. Olgin. Originally published 1929 by International Publishers Co., Inc.

10 Volkogonov, D. (1994). *Lenin: A New Biography*. New York, NY: The Free Press. Translation copyright 1994 Harold Shukman. pp. 483-484.

11 Rummel, R. J. (May 1, 2005). "The Red Plague." Retrieved March 23, 2010 from http://www.hawaii.edu/powerkills/commentary.htm.

12 Ibid., 7, p. 9.

13 Cortois, S., Werth, N., Panné, J., Paczkowski, K., & Margolin, J. (1999). *The Black Book of Communism*. Boston, MA: Harvard College. First printed in 1997 as *Le Livre Noir du Communisme*. Paris, FR: Editions Robert Laffont, S.A. p. 2.

14 Ibid., 7, p. 79.

15   Rummel, R. J. (2002). "20th Century Democide." Retrieved May 3, 2009 from http://www.hawaii.edu/powerkills/20th.htm

16   Ibid., 13, p. 95.

17   Ibid., 13, pp. 159-168.

18   The History Place (2000). "Stalin's Forced Famine 1932-33." Retrieved May 19, 2011 from http://www.historyplace.com/worldhistory/genocide/stalin.htm.

19   Dolot, M. (1987). *Execution by Hunger: The Hidden Holocaust*. New York, NY: W. W. Norton and Company. pp. 14-15.

20   Kravchenko, V. (1946). *I Chose Freedom: The Personal and Political Life of a Soviet Official*. New York, NY: Charles Scribner Sons. pp. 118-119.

21   Ibid., pp. 130-131.

22   Famine in Ukraine, 1932-1933. (1986), Canadian Institute of Ukrainian Studies, University of Alberta, 1986. p. 85.

23   Muggeridge, M. (1982). *The Green Stick*. Hopkins, MN: Olympic Marketing Corporation. p. 257.

24   Muggeridge, M. (1987). *Winter in Moscow*. Grand Rapids, MI: Eerdmans. xiv.

25   Yushchenko, V. (2007). "Holodomor". From the Official Website of President of Ukraine, Victor Yushchenko. Retrieved July 3, 2011 from http://www.president.gov.ua/en/news/8296.html.

26   Sábado (December 10, 2011). "Holodomor: Genocide by Starvation." Retrieved January 15, 2012 from http://talcana.

blogspot.com/2011/12/holodomor-el-genocidio-olvidado. html. Used by permission.

27 Grathwohl, L. (1982). "No Place to Hide: the Strategy and Tactics of Terrorism". Video Documentary. View video clip at http://wn.com/ Larry_Grathwohl on_Bill_Ayers_and_the_ Weather _Underground (Read transcript at http://lib.store. yahoo.net/lib/realityzone /noplacetohide.pdf)

8. FREEDOM AND FREE ENTERPRISE

1 Williams, T. C. (February 6, 2011). "Ronald Reagan's Farewell Address." Retrieved July 26, 2012 from http://republicanre-defined.com/2011/02/06/ronald-reagans-farewell-address/

REFERENCES

Bernays, E. (2005). *Propaganda*. Brooklyn, NY: IG Publishing. Originally published 1928.

Bernstein, E. (9161). *Evolutionary Socialism: A Criticism and Affir-mation*. New York, NY: Random House.

Boudreaux, D. (2001). "Human Creativity: Resources Don't Exist Until Humans Make Them Useful." The Freeman-Ideas on Liberty, March 2001, Volume: 51. Issue: 3.

Brooks, A. (2007). *Who Really Cares: The Surprising Truth About Compassionate Conservatism*, New York, NY: Basic Books, Perseus Books Group. Originally published 2006 in hard-cover by Basic Books.

Butler, A. (1980). Josiah Warren and the Sovereignty of the Indi-vidual. *The Journal of Libertarian Studies*, Vol. IV, No. 4.

Cortois, S., Werth, N., Panné, J., Paczkowski, K., & Margolin, J. (1999). *The Black Book of Communism*. Boston, MA: Harvard College. First printed in 1997 as *Le Livre Noir du Communisme*. Paris, FR: Editions Robert Laffont, S.A. 2.

Dickinson, J. (1801). *The Political Writings of John Dickinson*. Wilmington, DE: Bonsal and Niles. Vol. I.

Dolot, M. (1987). *Execution by Hunger: The Hidden Holocaust*. New York, NY: W. W. Norton and Company. 14-15.

Durant, W. & Durant, A. (1967). *The Story of Civilization*. Vol. X, Rousseau and Revolution. New York, NY: Simon and Schuster.

Gratwohl, L. (1982). "No Place to Hide: the Strategy and Tactics of Terrorism". Video Documentary. View video clip at http://wn.com/ Larry_Grathwohl on_Bill_Ayers_and_the_ Weather _Underground (Read transcript at http://lib.store. yahoo.net/lib/realityzone /noplacetohide.pdf)

Gower, R. (1987). *The New Manners and Customs of Bible Times*. Chicago, IL: The Moody Bible Institute of Chicago.

Kravchenko, V. (1946). *I Chose Freedom: The Personal and Political Life of a Soviet Official*. New York, NY: Charles Scribner Sons. 130-131.

Lambert, L. (1981). *Israel: The Unique Land, The Unique People*. Carol Stream, IL: Tyndale House Living Books.

LeBon, G. (1925). *The Crowd*. New York, NY: The Macmillan Company.

Lenin, V. (2004). *Collected Works of V. I. Lenin Completely Revised Edited and Annotated Part 20*. Whitefish, MT: Kessinger

Publishing. Translated by Joshua Kunitz and Moissaye J. Olgin. Originally published 1929 by International Publishers Co., Inc.

Lenin, V. (2004). *Collected Works of V. I. Lenin Completely Revised Edited and Annotated Part 20.* Whitefish, MT: Kessinger Publishing. Translated by Joshua Kunitz and Moissaye J. Olgin. Originally published 1929 by International Publishers Co., Inc.

Miller, T. & Holmes, K. (2009)."Economic freedom and standard of living." 210 Index of Economic Freedom (Washington, D.C.: The Heritage Foundation and Dow Jones & Company, Inc. 2010) at heritage.org/index: World Bank, World Development Indicators Online (November 10, 2009). Retrieved September 4, 2011 from http://publications.worldbank.org/WDI

Postrel, V. (1998). *The Future and Its Enemies: The Growing Conflict Over Creativity, Enterprise, and Progress.* New York, NY: The Free Press, a Division of Simon & Schuster, Inc.

Redleaf, A. and Vigilante, R. (2010). *Panic: The Betrayal of Capitalism by Wall Street and Washington.* Minneapolis, MN: Richard Vigilante Books. 8.

Rummel, R. J. (2002). "20th Century Democide." Retrieved May 3, 2009 from http://www.hawaii.edu/powerkills/20th.htm.

Rummel, R. J. (2004). *Death by Government.* Brunswick, NJ: Transaction Publishers. Originally published 1994.

Rummel, R. J. (1993). "How Many did Communist Regimes Murder?" Unpublished essay, Retrieved September 12, 2011from http://www.hawaii.edu/power kills/com.art.htm

Rummel, R. J. (2007). *Power Kills: Democracy as a Method of Non-violence*. Brunswick, NJ: Transaction Publishers. Originally published in 1997.

Rummel, R. J. (2007). *The Blue Book of Freedom*. Nashville, TN: Cumberland House Publishing. 11-16.

Simon, J. (1996). *The Ultimate Resource 2*. Princeton, N.J.: Princeton University Press. 23-40, 162-197.

Smith, R. (2002). *Adam Smith and the Origins of American Free Enterprise*. New York, NY: St. Martin's Press.

Sowell, T. (2009). *Intellectuals and Society*. New York, NY: Basic Books.

Sterling, C. (1982). *The Terror Network*. New York, NY: Berkeley Books. Originally published in 1981.

Stossel, J. (April 4,2011). "Government creates poverty." Washington Examiner. Monday, October 3, 2011. Retrieved October 3, 2011 from http://washingtonexaminer.com/opinion/ columnists/2011 /04/american-indians-demonstrate-how- government-help-creates-poverty?sms_ss=twitter&at_xt=4 dbafffcc9b29ca4,0.

Thatcher, M. (1976). From an interview with journalist Llew Gardner for Thames television's *This Week* program on November

5, 1976. Retrieved July 17, 2011 from http://www.margaret thatcher.org /speeches/displaydocument.asp?docid =102953

The Story Of Stuff, Referenced and Annotated Script. Retrieved September 2, 2010 from http://www.storyofstuff. com/ pdfs/ annie_ leonard_ footnoted_script.pdf.

Tocqueville, A. (2010). American Institutions and their Influence. With notes by Hon. John C. Spencer. New York, NY: A. S. Barnes and Co. Originally Cincinnati, OH: H.W. Derby & company, 1851.

Vander Laan, R. (2009). *Life and Ministry of the Messiah Discovery Guide*. Grand Rapids, MI: Zondervan.

Valdnieks, K. (Producer) & Snore, E. (Director), Daugavvanags, E. (Cinematography) (2010). The Soviet Story [DVD]. Latvia: SIA Labvakar.

Volkogonov, D. (1994). *Lenin: A New Biography*. New York, NY: The Free Press. Translation copyright 1994 by Harold Shukman.

Webster, N. (1828). *An American Dictionary of the English Language*. New York, NY: S. Converse. s.v. "property."

Wesley, J. (1991). *John Wesley's Sermons: An Anthology*. The Use of Money (1760). Nashville, TN: Abingdon Press.

Williams, T. C. (February 6, 2011). "Ronald Reagan's Farewell Address." Retrieved July 26, 2012 from http://republicanre-defined.com/2011/02/06/ronald-reagans-farewell-address/

CPSIA information can be obtained at www.ICGtesting.com
Printed in the USA
LVOW130316101012

302176LV00001B/10/P